"Bromleigh McCleneghan offers a provocative alternative to the tired conversations about sex in Christian culture, and all this from a deeply faithful and coherent engagement of Biblical texts and theological resources. I love her exploration of the central theme of love and how we embody it at so many levels in our connections—sex is much more than a behavior but a creative expression of a passionate God. Read *Good Christian Sex* if you desire a broader and practical conversation about sex, and a redemptive way of living out intimacy in all our relationships."

—Rev. Mihee Kim-Kort, author of *Yoked: Stories of a Clergy Couple in Marriage, Ministry, and Family*

"I was cynical of any book with 'sex' and 'Christian' in the same title. I read them before and knew the formula—dish out mortal shame, add fanciful gender stereotypes, and mix in some unrealistic puritanical expectations. But Bromleigh McCleneghan defied my worries with *Good Christian Sex* and left me with a faithful celebration of intimacy and pleasure. From a first sexual encounter to decades of marriage, McCleneghan's wisdom guides us through the nature of love."

—Carol Howard Merritt, pastor and columnist for the *Christian Century*

"In seminary, a professor asked where we'd learned about sex. Nobody in that group of churchy young adults mentioned church. McCleneghan has written the book we've needed all along; it's funny, honest, vulnerable, intelligent and challenging, and loving. It's for friends, lovers, partners, spouses, pastors, parents, and, very likely, you."

—Rev. Heidi Neumark, pastor at Trinity Lutheran Church and author of *Hidden Inheritance: Family Secrets, Memory, and Faith*

"*Good Christian Sex* is an important corrective to the unhealthy ways we imagine bodies, pleasure, and sin. Our conceptions of sexuality are mostly tied up in the traditions of religion, and Bromleigh is a wonder at untying difficult knots. I will be passing this along to friends."

—Rev. Julian "J.Kwest" DeShazier, senior minister at University Church Chicago and adjunct professor at University of Chicago Divinity School and McCormick Theological Seminary

"*Good Christian Sex* shows what open-minded, sex-positive encounters with the holy can and should look like. McCleneghan's tour de force is a reckoning with Christian tradition and an absolute delight to read. A must-read for anyone who wants to engage their heart, soul, and body."

—Rabbi Danya Ruttenberg, editor of *The Passionate Torah: Sex and Judaism*

"In *Good Christian Sex*, Bromleigh McCleneghan might surprise you. She might even offend you. But she will never pander, and she will never condescend. She's like an uncommonly wise, witty, and faithful big sister, telling you just enough of her own story to help you figure out the contours of your own. I can't imagine a more liberating invitation for Christians to receive the good and gracious gift of sexuality."

—Katherine Willis Pershey, associate minister of First Congregational Church and author of *Any Day a Beautiful Change* and *Very Married: Field Notes on Love & Fidelity*

Good Christian Sex

Good Christian Sex

Why Chastity Isn't the Only Option— And Other Things the Bible Says About Sex

Bromleigh McCleneghan

HarperOne
An Imprint of HarperCollinsPublishers

HarperOne

All scripture quotations, unless otherwise indicated, are taken from the *New Revised Standard Version Bible* (NRSV), copyright © 1989 National Council of the Churches of Christ in the United States of America. Used by permission. All rights reserved. Verses marked CEB are from the Common English Bible®, CEB® Copyright © 2010, 2011 by Common English Bible™. Used by permission. All rights reserved worldwide.

Grateful acknowledgment is given to the following for the use of their work in this publication:

"I Did Think, Let's Go About This Slowly" from *Felicity* by Mary Oliver, published by The Penguin Press New York. Copyright © 2015 by Mary Oliver. Reprinted by permission of The Charlotte Sheedy Literary Agency Inc. "Man in Space" from *The Art of Drowning*, by Billy Collins, © 1995. Reprinted by permission of the University of Pittsburgh Press. Excerpt from "Victoria's Secret" from *Picnic, Lightning*, by Billy Collins, © 1998. Reprinted by permission of the University of Pittsburgh Press.

HarperCollins books may be purchased for educational, business, or sales promotional use. For information, please email the Special Markets Department at SPsales@harpercollins.com.

FIRST EDITION

Library of Congress Cataloging-in-Publication Data

Names: McCleneghan, Bromleigh, author.
Title: Good Christian sex: why chastity isn't the only option--and other things the Bible says about sex / Bromleigh McCleneghan.
Description: FIRST EDITION. | San Francisco: HarperOne, 2016.
Identifiers: LCCN 2016011726 (print) | LCCN 2016013053 (ebook) | ISBN 9780062428592 (pbk.) | ISBN 9780062428608 (ebook)
Subjects: LCSH: Sex--Religious aspects--Christianity.
Classification: LCC BT708 .M4176 2016 (print) | LCC BT708 (ebook) | DDC 241/.664--dc23
LC record available at http://lccn.loc.gov/2016011726

19 20 21 22 LSC (H) 10 9 8 7 6 5 4

To Josh, as a sign of my vow,
with all that I have, and all that I am.

Contents

Introduction

On Sex and Christians

oston student apartments are hot in the summer—rare
is the window-unit AC offered to subletters; infinite
are the fourth-floor walk-ups. Summer nights are best
spent out—listening to a free concert at the Hatch Shell along
the river, or something on the Commons. But if there's nothing to do or see, no rooftop parties to attend, an evening can
be whiled away on the phone with a friend while alternately
drinking an ice water and allowing the sweating glass to drip
down on your own sweating arms for a moment of relief.

I learned these things about Boston in the summer
months before I turned twenty. Armed with an internship
at our local NPR affiliate and a part-time job in retail, I lived
in an apartment, on my own, for the first time ever. I loved

it, despite the heat. On one such sultry night a friend from high school called with a question. We hadn't spoken in ages, hadn't been close in years. She called for advice. "Should I sleep with my boyfriend?"

I was surprised by her question. Surprised she was asking, surprised she was asking *me*. I thought this was a pretty personal question, and one she could probably answer better for herself than I could.

We talked for a bit. *How long have you been together? Do you want to? Do you love him?*

Finally she made it clear why I was being asked. I was a Christian, as was she, and she wanted my opinion as such. I'm also a preacher's kid, and presumably had some insider authority on how to make such decisions faithfully.

I don't know if our surprise was mutual when she realized that neither I nor my very marvelous, very faithful parents were particularly opposed to sex outside of marriage. Sex among young teenagers, sex with inappropriate or nonconsenting partners, sex had by me—those were things my parents were not wild about, even against. But sex—even if it happened between people who weren't married—that wasn't such a terrible thing. We had family friends who were gay and partnered, and we had known couples who had lived together before marrying. These things happened, and they were not at the center of our moral concern as a family.

That's not to say that we didn't have moral concerns as a family. My parents are politically engaged, care passionately about poverty and peace and women's rights, about equality and freedom and justice. I was probably the only kid in my third-grade class who could explicate the reasons why

Michael Dukakis was the better candidate for president, the only one with opinions (however borrowed) about the arms race and the death penalty.

We went to church and I heard the gospel proclaimed week in and week out, and I heard that institutionalized gambling overburdens the poor, and that in some parts of the country people don't have access to clean drinking water and garbage pickup, much less good schools and health care, and that guns are, in the words of the grandfather in *Witness*, "for the taking of human life," and thus to be despised.

I heard about Jesus and Paul and Abraham and Sarah and Mary and John and Peter. I heard about John Wesley and Søren Kierkegaard, Paul Tillich and Reinhold Niebuhr, Martin Luther King, Jr., and Phyllis Trible and Peter Berger (and his *A Rumor of Angels*). I learned the stories and the songs of the faith. I learned that our Christology was high and our God was good. I learned that we are called to grow ever more perfect in love, but that sin is real, in individuals and in society, and our hope is eschatological. I learned that holiness is both personal and social.

But I very rarely learned about sex or romantic love in the context of church, or God. Agape, yes. But eros? Not on your life.

My parents were not too prudish or too proper to speak of such things. Or, at least, they were not too prudish or too proper to hand me books about such things.

We had several "how babies are made" books available on our bookshelves at home, including one with the most amazing color photography of fetal development. As I got a little older, I was offered a copy of Joanna Cole's *Asking About Sex and Growing Up*—the text was enthralling enough, but the book also featured illustrations by the same guy who'd done all the drawing for my beloved editions of Beverly Cleary's Ramona books. While it was a bit odd to see a character resembling Ramona's friend Howie nude and gradually maturing, the familiar illustrations led to my dawning understanding of human sexual development as just a normal everyday part of life.

A normal everyday part of life that wasn't coming my way anytime soon. I was a late bloomer, straight up and down for years, with my still-tiny features dwarfed by a series of huge, brightly colored pairs of glasses. My failure to fill out *anything*, even the most modest of training bras, rendered "sex and growing up" an unattainable and thus deeply alluring goal.

Maybe my parents didn't push the sex talk with me because I was so obviously awkward for so very long. All I know is that my mother handed me this wonderful, nurturing, factual book, with the vague instruction to "just read what applies to you." She probably meant "just do the chapters about menstruation and breasts," but I'd been a reader for years by then and devoured the whole thing. I read the chapters about girls and boys and crushes and secondary sex characteristics, but also about masturbation and birth control and "going all the way."

Shortly thereafter, on the endlessly long ride from our hometown in suburban Chicago to Washington, DC, to visit my grandparents, I'd finished all the books I'd brought along, worn out the batteries on my Walkman, and was bored, bored, bored. I could feel the whine rising in my chest, when my mom told me to reach into the backseat and dig out something from the big bag of novels she'd brought along.

In this bag was probably a wide assortment of paperback editions of literary fiction. My mother's affinity for the "Books" section of the Sunday paper predates most of her other loves, and it was through her that I was introduced to great contemporary authors, especially great women writers, in my early teens. I read Barbara Kingsolver, Jane Smiley, Anne Tyler, Margaret Atwood, and Louise Erdrich.

That day, though, I homed in on a trashy romance novel— the sort with a virginal woman busting out of a ripped petticoat or bustier, swooning in the arms of a muscular man with equally long, flowing hair. It was most likely a castoff from my paternal grandmother, something she'd picked up in the thrift shop where she volunteered. At that age—late elementary school or early junior high—I wasn't really ready for Atwood or Erdrich. Their vocabularies were beyond me. The content of the cheesy paperback was risqué, but the reading level was closer to my own.

I held it up to show to my mom. "Can I read this one?"

"I guess. Just make sure you skip any parts you don't think you should be reading."

And that is how, in the back of my parents' minivan, with my parents and sisters on a family trek across the Pennsylvania Turnpike, I came to be acquainted with oral sex.

I will tell you: it sounded awesome, and made the deciphering of the increasingly obscure euphemisms for human anatomy well worth the effort.

Now, I don't know if this is a particularly common experience, or that I'd recommend this strategy of sex education—the "take and read" approach—to just anyone. I was shy and awkward, flat-chested and bespectacled, and had largely internalized the Dorothy Parker adage that "men seldom make passes at girls who wear glasses" years before I first encountered her work as a freshman in high school. I was also generally supervised; I was either babysitting or being actively parented, so there was no opportunity for me to get "into trouble." Knowing about the existence of sex acts was simply that; I was in no danger of getting any hands-on (ahem) experience.

And that time of waiting and wondering proved critically important: I had the opportunity to reflect on what I wanted and what I dreamed of—from sex and from relationships. Thus, what my reading taught me, I wouldn't trade for the world. From *Asking About Sex and Growing Up,* I gleaned that we all go through the joys and pains of growing up, that our bodies can be sources of pain and pleasure, that boys and girls and men and women have desires, that sex can have consequences, but that there are also ways to mitigate at least some of those consequences through, for example, the proper and regular use of condoms.

From the trashy romance novels, I learned that sex was supposed to be mutually pleasurable, and something that grew out of a relationship of love. I also learned the some-what misleading (who would have thought?) lesson that sex was always both culmination and beginning, a moment of vulnerability that changed everything, irrevocably for both partners, from that point onward. Sometimes sex is not both those things; sometimes it changes very little.

The literary fiction served as an important corrective as I

got older and got to be a better reader. Sex was complicated, and so were human relationships. Sometimes marriages were awful; sometimes sex was about power and not love; sometimes the sex was the best part of a relationship; sometimes things went well and love grew and grew.

And then, in the middle of all of that reading, I fell in love. We'll have more on first loves later, but in those late adolescent years, I learned that all three of the "texts" I'd been basing my assumptions on proclaimed some measure of truth.

Where, though, was my faith in all of this?

My family and I were mainline Protestants, and as with many mainline Protestants, even good, highly churched ones, human sexuality wasn't tied to my nascent theology and ethics. I know this isn't the case for every tradition or denomination, and that there are many Christians who handle the topic differently than we did. I knew my parents weren't keen on my sleeping with anyone—and I wasn't ready to for quite a while—but I assumed that had more to do with their being my parents and icked out about my sexual maturation than anything in particular to do with God. My dad got mad when I was late for curfew; my mom recommended that I think long and hard about sex with my high school boyfriend, because it would make it harder to break up when the time came. The theological import of all this for my pastor father was never particularly explicit.

But if absolute abstinence outside of marriage wasn't exactly a pressing question or concern for my sisters and me, other things were. If we were going to have sex, were we going to practice safer sex? Were we going to be faithful within the contexts of our relationships? Were we going to be good friends? Were we going to be honest and loving and gracious and kind? Did we have the resources—the self-knowledge and resilience—we needed to guard against being bullied or guilted into doing something we didn't want to do or weren't ready for?

So a few years later when my friend called asking for advice, I might have been living on my own for the first time, but the questions I was ready to ask her as we talked through her decision were not contrary to the ethic with which I was raised. Still, despite the ubiquitous influence of the church community on my childhood, I was hard-pressed to think of how this particular decision might be affected by the common faith we professed. Many Christians in this country hear a singular ethic from their faith communities—absolute abstinence outside of marriage, never abortion, no birth control (and no being gay)—and simply disengage, disconnecting their sex lives from their lives of faith.

That wasn't the ethic with which I was raised, but the mainline churches tend to prioritize privacy and personal discernment around issues about bodies and relationships and instead bring the Bible to bear on broader issues of society, asking questions of faith that are far more abstract than "Should I sleep with my boyfriend?" This may well be because we in the mainline church trust folks to know their own contexts best and we'd rather not even know, lest we judge.

There are some significant limitations to that approach, though. I knew to always use a condom and make sure my

partners and I were regularly tested for STIs, but I didn't always know what other criteria might help me make *emotionally* or *spiritually* healthy decisions. These limitations have
much broader impact than the ordering of my early relationships. There's the general way mainline churches can seem
out of touch with the personal battles of members' lives, and
there's also a somewhat irresponsible tendency to leave the
discovery of needed resources, emotional and informational,
to fate, and to implicitly suggest that those who need help
can't ask for it from the community. So many churches say
and do nothing toward helping people form faithful understandings of what it means to be in relationship with others. We did get some sex ed at my church, but it was mostly
biology. Thus, I had the logistics, but not the ethics; the
information, but not the wisdom. My peers whose parents
didn't have a healthy understanding of sexuality, or the will
or wherewithal to communicate one to their kids, were often
lost without a guide in the wilderness of adolescence and
early adulthood. "Don't ask / don't tell" is a lousy strategy for
making disciples.

Frederick Buechner, a writer and pastor, has a series of
books that read like little dictionaries of the Christian tradition. His definition of sex, in the book *Wishful Thinking*,
begins like this:

> Contrary to Mrs. Grundy, sex is not sin. Contrary
> to Hugh Hefner, it's not salvation either. Like nitro-
> glycerin, it can be used either to blow up bridges or
> heal hearts.[1]

I, like many American teenagers and young adults, took the Hugh Hefner line of thinking for a long time. There are, of course, a whole host of American teenagers and young adults who have taken the former view at the strong urging of their parents and churches. *Sex is dangerous and shameful and sinful and a tool of the devil until that day you're married, at which point it is awesome and a gift from God. Good luck!*

What we all tend to miss is Buechner's point that sex and love are both/and—and they are rightly about bodies and souls, hearts and hormones. And, for Buechner, sex and love are also about sin and salvation, about the nature of God and Christian discipleship. Though my church talked very rarely about human sexuality, I grew up to know that the gospel that was preached calls us to see these paradoxes in our lives—that the best things involve some risk, that love is an easy yoke—and to reach out in faith.

I've wanted to have this book in my possession since that sweaty, sultry night in the middle of college, my first summer away from home, when my friend called. Because when she called, I could help her to make a healthy decision, but I couldn't help her make the connection between her nascent love for this guy and her love for God. I didn't know how; I didn't have the theological practice.

I've wanted this book for years, to share in conversation with parishioners and friends, to help me sort out how Christians can think about our romantic and sexual lives— which are so very vital—in the light of our faith. I've waited, and I've read a lot, and finally gave up and am writing it myself.

There are, of course, plenty of Christian books about sex.

Some might say there are too many. There are spiritual and theological memoirs, and there are ethics handbooks. There are screeds and polemics and manifestos. There are complex texts, written for academic audiences. The handbooks are often useful, if you can get through them; the theological texts, too. They manage what most of the polemics do not: those who write in ethics almost always tell you what ideas they're taking as given, or how they've decided upon their norms.

In some ways, that's what this book attempts to do: to lay out some of the theological and ethical questions that arise in your average, everyday experience of adult sexuality, and to walk readers through those discussions in a clear and engaging way.

But boring, technical, humorless writing about sex and love is antithetical to what I think sex is all about. So are esoteric texts on a topic that just about everyone has some experience of; books about love and sex should be accessible, I think.

Many of the memoirs are accessible, but their theological convictions are often idiosyncratic. My hope is to, in the words of my math teacher husband, Josh, "show my [theological] work" in the midst of reflecting on my stories.

I am also quite aware that not everyone in the world is all that interested in my personal life, and there are many aspects about my romantic and sexual history that are decidedly privileged. I'm a straight white woman, born to educated feminist Christians, who worked hard never ever to shame me for becoming the person God is calling me to be. I'm able-bodied and reasonably attractive by society's current standards, and my fertility is ridiculously, and unusually, responsive to both birth control and the lack thereof.

As someone who's spent a good number of years talking to parishioners, students, and friends, while I'm aware of the things that make my experience both particular and privileged, I'm also increasingly convinced of the broader resonance of the theological and ethical norms I've come to hold. That is to say, while the details are sometimes different, gay or straight, trans-or cisgender, most of us want to love and be loved, to find relationships in which we can be ourselves and also experience the thrill of desire. I know there are those who were taught that "good Christian sex" could only ever be for straight, married people, and it's my hope that this book, with its rather different argument, will resonate with them as well. As a pastor, as a Christian, I hope the simple acknowledgment that there may be more than one acceptable—holy and just—way to live as sexual beings is a blessing and an invitation to those who have been taught that God's way is singular and exclusive.

In this book, I draw on my own experience, but also on the experiences of lots of other people. For the truth is, I was a shy late bloomer, and my husband and I got together (also on a sweaty summer night, this time in Chicago) when I was twenty-three, and almost all of the experiences I had in the intervening years were, if not always positive, at least not traumatic. To broaden my knowledge base (and to mask the experiences of those I've learned through in confidential pastoral relationships), I posted a survey on Facebook and encouraged friends and colleagues to disseminate it during

Lent of 2014. Most of the questions were open-ended, even "What is your gender?" I wanted to hear people's stories— about first times, about the relationship between love and sex, about the ages of respondents' sexual debuts. Over 330 people responded. There was so much that amazed me about the stories I heard, but the most amazing thing was that anonymous people shared their intimate thoughts and experiences with me. As each response came in, I felt gratitude.

Some of those people's stories are present in the following chapters. Because of the narrative nature of the survey, I didn't even attempt to quantify the results. I simply wanted to know whether or not most of the things that felt true to me felt true to others. I wanted to know what questions people are asking about love, sex, God, and church.

Throughout the book, I attempt to speak to a number of the expressed concerns of my survey respondents. In the first chapter, I try to make theological sense of pleasure, as something that is a part—a wonderful and important part—of being human, and something we encounter from our earliest years. Chapter two chronicles some of my first experiences of desire as *good*, in conversation with the Bible and some contemporary theologians, and asks that we think about virginity and sexual initiation as complex things. Chapter three looks at norms of sexual ethics, and asks about both the authority of the Bible and what, *exactly*, was at stake in that sophomore year serial hookup. Chapter four reflects on how God works in the world and whether or not single Christians have to be celibate. Chapter five considers modesty, nudity, and what it means to be vulnerable with other people. Chapter six is about intimacy of a variety of sorts. Chapter seven is about "history"—what we are to do with the great joys and deep injuries of our pasts, especially for those who are survivors of abuse. Chapter eight is about fidelity, and lust, and what makes being faithful worth it, and so hard. Chapter nine, the last one, considers how it is that we know whether it's time to break it off, or make a go of it, and the story of Jesus feeding the five thousand makes a somewhat unexpected appearance. My hope is that these chapters, while certainly not inclusive of all topics or experiences, will nonetheless cast a broad and deep enough net that many people can locate themselves within its pages, even if they're dudes, or gay, or what have you.

Writing this book has been an opportunity to reach back through the years and consider what I might have told my friend, not just about sex and relationships, but about God, and the Bible, and how all these things are tied together. This book is an opportunity, I hope, for readers to ask questions about their own relationships and practices, so that maybe, just maybe, they can experience the grace of God, and grow in love of self, God, and other.

For my friend contemplating whether or not to take the next step with her boyfriend, things were relatively straightforward, once we set aside the assumption that she could not, should not, have sex outside of marriage. She loved and trusted him. I don't know if they had sex for the first time subsequent to that phone call, but they're married now, and have been for a while, so I'm assuming that they did eventually. My hope is that whenever they had sex for the first time, it was holy, and wonderful, just as my hope for all people is that we know love, joy, holiness, and pleasure in these lives God has given us. I'm hoping this book can help make a difference to that end, even though it's nonfiction, lacks pictures of Ramona and Howie, and has only a very limited number of ripped bodices and ridiculous euphemisms. It will, to be fair, have a lot more God.

Chapter One

"My Favorite Feel"

Pleasure as a Gift from God

W hen I was a preteen, my parents handed me a book to introduce me to the world of puberty and sex, a book that included a chapter called "Touching Feels Good."

Of all the things I remember about my childhood, of all the clear memories I have of playing Legos and Barbies and lip-synching to *Cats* and Smokey Robinson for audiences of playmates and parents, I cannot recall whether this formative text, and that particular chapter, provided me with new information or the affirmation of something I had already experienced.

Long before I ever had a sexual partner, I discovered first-hand[1] that humans are wired to experience sexual pleasure.

Wired to experience, and *enjoy*, sexual pleasure.

I know that for some people this topic is morally fraught, but as a teenager, I was never really concerned about other people's thoughts on the morality of pursuing sexual pleasure with oneself, perhaps because the book I read told me that it's "normal to touch your sex organs for pleasure,"[2] and "whichever way makes you happy is the right way for you."[3] As a kid and later as a teenager, I *was* intensely concerned with what was normal, with fitting in, and thus was grateful to hear that, in this regard, I was like most people. I was normal.

For many, many Christians, though, the pursuit of pleasure—generally, or sexual pleasure specifically—is a fraught thing, even when it's pleasure without a partner. The idea that "if something feels right, it is right" is deeply suspect; strains of Christianity have long thought of temptation to pleasure as the work of the, well, the Tempter. How we think about pleasure, and, in turn, about sin and incarnation, will certainly impact our understanding of what makes for "good Christian sex." Looking specifically at masturbation (an aurally unpleasant word of uncertain etymology—let's call it self-stimulation instead, shall we?), which is partnerless sex, allows us to consider a whole host of topics, including cultural myths, pseudoscience, the differences between men and women, pornography, and self-harm.

Still, it's kind of awful to talk about, isn't it? This is the chapter in which I would love to quote everyone else and use every evasive narrative tactic I can muster, because I am perfectly content with readers knowing that I have slept with some people, but not that teenage me was keenly aware of how I liked to be touched before I ever got around to having a partner.

Why is that? I imagine my reticence, my embarrassment (I am blushing in the Corner Bakery, where I type), has a great deal to do with the cultural baggage around self-stimulation—in pursuing pleasure with and for oneself alone. But it's important, and so before we move to sexual relationships with others, let's start with the idea of "pleasure" itself and unpack how it has been understood culturally and theologically. We'll look, too, at the biblical story Christians used to cite as a prohibition against solo sex, and see if it can provide any insight into how we are to include seeking after pleasure in our pursuit of a faithful, Christian life.

MY RETICENCE TO speak about pleasure and the solo pursuit of it is not just because it's embarrassing as all get-out. It's also because I'm a woman talking about the solo pursuit of pleasure. Much of our cultural conversation around sex and pleasure is highly gendered. Think about slang terms for masturbation—like "wanking" in England, or "jacking off" in the States—which are insults in the nominative: *That guy's a wanker; what a jack-off.*

Those classy insults are almost always lodged at men. In the last century or so, the idea that the pursuit of sexual pleasure is solely the provenance of men and boys came into wider acceptance, on a variety of fronts. First-wave (white) feminists and suffragists encouraged the notion that (white)[4] women were more likely to be the moral protectors of the home, practitioners of self-restraint and resolve, who could encourage (or guilt) men into denying their baser selves (and thus should be given the vote for the betterment of society).[5] Self-proclaimed Christian fundamentalists asserted the more genteel, fragile nature of women and the need for men to claim their strength and spiritual headship, to rein in their sexual instincts and live as godly men.

Feminism grew and changed as the years passed and the nature of the equality of the sexes was articulated in new ways, while fundamentalist Christians dug in their heels on gender difference. Desire for sexual pleasure among women either did not exist or was a sign of deep confusion about what a true or biblical woman was supposed to be like, was created to be.

Maybe I don't feel comfortable copping to self-pleasure because somewhere, deep down, I think it's not okay for women to want sex. If that were the case, I wouldn't be alone.

I asked my survey respondents about their experience, if any, of masturbation in childhood and adolescence. *Did you . . . ? If so, how did you understand that act? (As shameful? Natural? Private? Awesome? Not interesting?)* Many, many of the respondents answered in the affirmative (a popular response was "yes, constantly!") and many answered "private and awesome." Some were not interested, some only started masturbating later, after they became sexually active. But no small number of women reported that they had for a long time been unaware that women could bring themselves to orgasm. That was "just a thing boys did."

One woman recalled being at a statewide leadership retreat as a teen, and the topic came up, as it does among teenagers late at night:

Someone brought up guys and the fact that they masturbate—and it was roundly agreed that girls wouldn't do that; they would never be so disgusting. I never confessed—but I've thought of that night many times and the perceived taboo of women's sexuality, and/or sexuality in general. The other girls were from the metro area; I was from the sticks.

In our culture, we are often made to understand that women and girls are not sexual beings, and are properly disgusted by sexual displays and acts. Any sexual interest we have is thus unnatural or strange, something to be embarrassed about. In much of Christian culture, too, particularly over the last 150 years in the United States, gender difference has been reinforced through prescriptions of "biblical manhood" and "biblical womanhood." This is a new-ish historical development; for a long time, the most familiar women in the Bible were (other than Mary, the mother of Jesus, sainted virgin) temptresses and prostitutes: Eve, Delilah, Jezebel, to name just a few. Feminist theologians have criticized both understandings of strict gender divisions, suggesting that women are ill-served by being offered only two ways of being in the world: Madonna or whore.

Outside of the Christian tradition, but in the West more generally, women were seen as the ones controlled by their bodies and passions; men were the coolheaded, spiritual ones in much of Western culture for centuries. Case in point: the word "hysterical," meaning unduly emotional, comes from the Latin and Greek words for uterus. Women were seen as uniquely susceptible to such feelings of hysteria, due to some dysfunction in their lady parts.

The more we learn about gender and sexuality, however, the more obvious it is that there is no clear demarcation between male and female, much less ideal personality types for each gender. There is incredible diversity, a host of intersex conditions, a spectrum upon which we spend our lives trying to locate ourselves. Some women love sex. Some men don't. Some folks only like sex under given conditions. But we're doing no one any favors by suggesting that women don't like sex and men are basically begging for it during every waking moment.

IT'S NOT JUST gender that makes the discussion of pleasure complicated. Human beings have long wondered about the connection between our bodies and our souls or spirits or characters. In the first half of the nineteenth century, when medicine and psychology were both emerging as scientific disciplines, there were yet a number of specious connections made between physiology and personality. Phrenology asserted that the shape of someone's head could indicate their character; certain common variations in facial features across races were understood to represent different strengths and weaknesses among groups of people.

In the early twentieth century, acne was seen as a side effect of masturbation and thus moral failing. Pity those turn-of-the-century teenagers, especially those with oily skin! Other children were told that touching themselves would lead to hairy palms or going blind . . . Obviously neither is true, but the persistence and dubious (or diverse?) origins of those superstitions suggest that we have long been in the business of shaming people for seeking pleasure. Do not do this strange, unnatural, bad thing, or there will be distressing consequences that will reveal your sin to others. You will be found out.

Why are we so ambivalent about our bodies? Why do people work so hard to pass that ambivalence on to their children? I used to lead a women's group at a church I served, and one day we got to talking about how our children refuse to allow us any privacy in the bathroom. Dealing with varied menstrual products with an audience is the worst. I'm not a particularly private person, but even that pushes my limits. Still, the most frustrating thing for these women was trying to explain away what their children were seeing. They used slang and euphemisms, and generally refused to explain that this was a natural way for a woman's body to work.

I confess, I've not come clean with my kids about all the details of sex yet—even the baby-making part; they know about sperm and eggs, but not the mechanism by which they meet. I don't think they're ready, though my oldest one is getting close. But menstruation? The topic seems terribly innocuous to me and yet it nonetheless caused these lovely and capable women to bend over backward trying to avoid telling their children the truth.

Are we channeling the spirit of those verses in Leviticus that lay out how menstruation renders a woman unclean and defiles anything she touches during that time of the month? Or the church fathers who believed that original sin was literally transmitted via semen and intercourse? Or the reformers Martin Luther and John Calvin, who proposed that human nature is totally corrupted and depraved and has been since Adam and Eve?

The influence of Augustine, fourth-century Bishop of Hippo, even on Christians who haven't read him, really can't be overstated. And before him, the influence of Plato on biblical writers and the first Christian theologians. Plato and other Greek schools of thought believed that existence was divided into matter and antimatter—material things and spiritual things. The spiritual things, the ideas, Truth and Beauty, those things were unchanging, pure, lovely, good. Bodies—which women seemed to have a harder time transcending by virtue of childbearing—were "profane," ever changing, subjective.

Augustine, early in his life, was very influenced by these schools of thought, and by a group known as the Manichaeans, who were similarly dualistic in their understanding of good and evil—matter was evil, spirit was good. Augustine thought being a Christian would require him to give up what was evil—or, at least, tainted by sin. He famously prayed, *Give me chastity and self-control, but not just yet.*[6] Augustine didn't ever go so far as Jerome, who thought lifelong celibacy ought to be normative for Christians, but he did tend to think sexual pleasure almost always involved turning away from God toward the desires of the body, even in marriage. But the bishop's career was long, and he came to understand sexuality differently over time. My friend Kyle,[7] who just finished writing a brilliant dissertation on Augustine, the Trinity, and Love, points out that "in his very late Genesis commentary, Augustine argues that sex and reproduction are normal and good, and Adam and Eve would have had sex and begotten children even in paradise. Alas, his reasoning is that if God's only goal for them was companionship, God would have created a second man instead of a woman."

(Oh, those church fathers! So timeless in some things, so ridiculously impacted by the biases of their own times in others.)

As much as those early Christians were influenced by body/soul dualism, however, the far more enduring theological conviction is that our bodies, souls, minds, and hearts are intertwined. That's the heart of Christian incarnational theology. God creates us in the divine image, creates us with bodies, creates us through earth and divine breath, creates us good. Jesus is fully human and fully divine; in these bodies, with these minds, we're both powerful and vulnerable.

The marveling poetry of Psalm 8 names the paradox across the centuries:

When I look at your heavens, the work of your fingers,
    the moon and the stars that you have established;
what are human beings that you are mindful of them,
    mortals that you care for them?
Yet you have made them a little lower than God,
    and crowned them with glory and honor.

(PSALM 8:3–5)

Our bodies are not base matter to be transcended, their needs ignored or denied in pursuit of holiness. They are us, gifts from God, though, indeed, mutable and mortal, prone to (in the words of the wonderful theologian Kris Culp) vulnerability and glory.

A CENTRAL THEOLOGICAL question over the years, however, is about the nature of human life—is it altogether sinful in light of the Fall?

The vast majority of people have sexual relationships at some point in their lives. And many people have engaged in self-stimulation at some point; by age twenty, 92 percent of men and two-thirds of women.[8] Infants have been known to touch themselves, as do young children "before the age of reason." They do it innocently, which challenges the idea that the pursuit of such pleasure is particularly sinful. Maybe it's just another human thing, like eating and sleeping.

If sexual pleasure is such a common—nearly universal—human experience, what makes a difference for people, what makes exploring these early theologians' work important, is how we interpret that pursuit of pleasure. Does it necessarily require turning away from God; does sexual pleasure always incite lust or incline us toward sin? Should we interpret that pursuit as sinful and worthy of shame, or as good and natural?

More pressingly, I wonder about the effects of teaching children that something that is natural and commonplace is sinful.

Theologian and ethicist Christine Gudorf would affirm Augustine's belief that sex and pleasure are part of God's good creation, but she points out that to claim that sex is a part of God's good creation is insufficient, given that a bunch of things that exist as parts of creation are decidedly *not* good. Hurricanes, drought, HIV and malaria, piranhas: those are part of creation but aren't high on anyone's list of celebrated phenomena.[9]

Nevertheless, she writes, "sexual pleasure can be argued as good for a much simpler, more commonsensical reason. It feels good. Like a hot tub for aching muscles, cool water on a hot day . . . sexual pleasure makes us feel good."

Pleasure, in fact, is itself a good. Not *the* good, but *a* good. Sexual pleasure is what Gudorf calls a "premoral good"— which means it should be understood as "one aspect of the general social good."[10] Moral discernment will help us to know when sexual pleasure needs to be sacrificed to other goods—but it is not in itself sinful or wrong or shameful. As human beings, Gudorf states, "we *need* pleasure; we need *body* pleasure."[11] We need experiences of pleasure just as surely as we need to limit our experiences of pain and suffering, for our bodies and for our souls.

Among my survey respondents, there were those who felt that the pursuit of pleasure, even as children, even without lust or partner, was a "sin against my chastity." But there were far more who, even before they knew how to make sense of what they were doing, even before they understood themselves as sexual beings, thought of what they were doing as special, good, private; one woman referred to it as "my favorite feel" when she was a child. Another, on realizing that she could make herself feel good—relaxed and lovely— considered self-stimulation "a gift from God."

That language gives me pause—we don't usually think about masturbation as a gift from God. But insofar as human beings need body pleasure, it is a safe (and pretty reliable) way to meet a very human need. Sounds like a gift from a benevolent creator, after all.

This is not to say, however, that chastity is no longer a virtue, or that pleasure ought to be pursued all the time without limit.

I love the writer Caitlin Moran. A broadsheet columnist in England who started out as a music critic, she writes about everything and nothing from a populist feminist perspective. She is hilarious.

I love the social consciousness Moran developed growing up poor and on welfare in the UK, and I love how she describes her adolescence and the fear and anxiety she had about becoming a woman. Her mother gave her neither instructive books featuring Ramona and Howie nor direct access to trashy romance novels; she assumed Caitlin and her sisters would "[pick] it all up from *Moonlighting*."[12]

Things change ever so slightly for the better after Cate's thirteenth birthday, when she is allowed an adult library card. She has recently fallen in love with Fletch-era Chevy Chase and she intends to check out the movie novelization so she can gaze lovingly at Chase's picture on the cover and imagine him stroking her face. She finds her book and, as an afterthought, picks up another she thinks is about horses. In fact, it's ridiculous smut and within the space of an afternoon and a couple of dozen pages she gains quite the education. This is "the key text that will translate 'new and unusual feelings' that [she has] been having into 'masturbating furiously and compulsively for the next four years.'"[13]

Moran dislikes the "m-word" as much as I do; its

pronunciation evokes definitions counter to her experience: "What I am doing, by way of contrast, is dreamlike, delicate, and soft—apart from the occasions where I have grown my nails too long and become so sore I have to repel my own advances for a few days."[14] It is, despite the dangers posed by overzealous attention to oneself, a perfect hobby: "It doesn't cost anything, I don't have to leave the house, and it isn't making me fat."[15]

It is a gift, the one thing about adolescence and the encroaching ambiguities of womanhood that she can enjoy and treasure.

Of course, her adolescent preoccupation with wooing herself is exactly what Christians, ancient and modern, are often afraid of. That our pursuit of pleasure will send us into ourselves, will turn us away from God. That we will give in to lust, fantasizing about others, and grow addicted.

In one popular Christian sex ed curriculum, the question of the morality of self-stimulation is raised: *Some Christians believe it is always wrong because it usually involves visualizing someone you're not married to . . . .* Plus, it's sexual stimulation outside of marriage. But other Christians, according to the curriculum, think it's normal. This view, however, is quickly countered with the contention that "it can easily become addictive and controlling." Entertaining sexual desires inevitably leads people to actions that are harmful or otherwise shameful.

The book I grew up with is not nearly so alarmist, stating:

> Masturbating a lot does not do any harm, but it
> may be a sign that you are trying to make yourself

feel better when you are tense or unhappy about
something. In that case, it is more important to try
to get help with that problem than it is to worry
about masturbating.[16]

Masturbating—straight-up sexual pleasure—is neither always good nor always bad. It is simply a part of being human that can be used to delight and comfort, or as a means
of avoidance and self-harm. But sexual pleasure does not in
and of itself harm, anger, or dishonor God.

In the sixth chapter of 1 Corinthians, the apostle Paul
rather famously charged early Christians to "shun fornication! . . . Do you not know that your body is a temple of
the Holy Spirit within you, which you have from God, and
that you are not your own? For you were bought with a
price; therefore glorify God in your body" (1 Corinthians
6:18–20). This passage is often cited as justification for
all kinds of abstinence, but I wonder if that's what Paul
meant.

Is it glorifying to God to deny our bodies—created good,
created by God—the things they need for health and joy?
Is a prohibition against all pleasure outside of very circum-
scribed circumstances like marriage—which for most folks,
who begin to sexually mature around thirteen but don't
marry until (on average) twenty-six, means more than a decade of frustrated need for release and desire for pleasure—
glorifying to God?

The second-century church father Irenaeus wrote, "the
glory of God is the human person fully alive." Not repressed,
shamed, afraid, or lonely. The glory of God is in human

beings living in the light of grace, in the presence of the good, the true, the beautiful, the holy.

Moran's description of her sexual awakening is just this— life is no longer drudgery; life is no longer terrifying. There is this soft, lovely, exciting thing and, importantly, "it feels like it will—eventually—somehow—I don't know how—and only if I attend to its lessons carefully—make me dress right, say the correct things, give me the impetus to leave the house and find whatever it is that's out there for me."[17]

CHRISTIANS ARE SIMILARLY called to attend carefully to the lessons of our sexuality. Because it is private, it can become isolating; because it is a balm, it can become a panacea; because it can be part of a healthy life, we often forget that it can be dangerous. My friend Kyle, the Augustine expert, points out that Augustine was not just some prudish stick-in-the-mud: "In the ancient world, sex almost always meant conception—that is, there was no reliable contraception— and childbearing was an extremely dangerous proposition for women (and still is in a lot of places)."

Chastity provided not just freedom from whatever host of sins you could toss under the umbrella of sexual immorality, but freedom from the potential of disease or death. Chastity was not about limitation for many—especially early Christian women in religious orders—but about new freedoms to live fully into grace.

Christians are called not to indulge their every desire—if we continued into adulthood with the masturbatory practices of adolescence no one would ever get any work done—but to attend to our desires as a part of living into grace. Attempting to repress or sublimate our desires and human needs, accepting the shame or condemnation of our humanity as embodied creatures, does not help us connect with God. In fact, it is there that we run into trouble.

Sexual and pornography addictions are real problems, and devastating in their consequences. Though they are notably not yet included in the DSM-V as diagnosable illnesses, they're obviously what we might call "adverse sexual behaviors." Contrary to the rhetoric of many Christian groups, however, it's not simply exposure to sexual material or tending to our desires that causes them. Untreated anxiety, depression, obsessive compulsive disorders, trauma, substance abuse, loneliness or isolation: these can contribute to unhealthy sexual behaviors, and those behaviors' growing in importance in one's life. Just like many folks with alcohol and drug problems use those substances to self-medicate underlying psychological issues, some folks use sex or porn. Just like kids and adolescents are more prone to develop unhealthy dependencies the younger they are when they start to use alcohol or drugs, early exposure to porn, especially intense porn on the Internet, can be more risky than when adults encounter it.

Video poker is like that, too. The rush from winning, from betting, from risking, affects our brains chemically— especially in those chemically impressionable adolescent years. But we rarely get so bent out of shape about kids getting addicted to gambling.

Removing the shame and isolation, treating underlying mental health issues, and preventing exposure to explicit materials, though, seem like much more effective responses to dealing with the evils of addiction and the bazillion-dollar pornography industry than attempting to get humans to rid themselves of a part of their humanity.

Indeed, Moran's concern about pornography is that there is too much *bad* porn out there: if there were more porn that highlighted what actual women actually enjoy, a whole range of sexual ills might be remedied, most especially unrealistic expectations among young men and false portrayals of how to bring a woman to orgasm (very few women like x, y, and z. For serious, gents). The problem with bad porn for Moran (other than the crimes periodically involved in making it) is that it leads to bad sex.

I'm significantly more ambivalent about pornography than Moran is, but I do believe that sexual pleasure is a wonderful thing, and that it can open us to others and the world in important ways. Knowing what gives us joy can help us to know how and where to seek it, and, just as critically, recognize something that's not satisfying, or joyful or good. Experiences of pleasure can also help us to relax, to gain confidence and the assurance we need to grow into healthy adults.

For most people, the pursuit of pleasure is a good they are able to hold alongside other goods. Moran grew out of her constant self-wooing. Same goes for most of the self-lovers in my survey. Gudorf also addresses the claim that masturbation invariably leads us inward, to isolation and sin.

Research shows that the practice of masturbation does not prevent men and women from seeking out

sexual partners. In fact, among women, it has become clear that women who have masturbated are
more likely to experience general sexual pleasure
and, in particular, orgasm [and thus connection
and satisfaction, I'd add] in partnered sex than are
women who have not masturbated. Rather than
finding that solitary sex is an obstacle to shared
sex, research suggests that solitary sex is helpful to
women in later partnered sex in a variety of ways.[18]

The Christian life, Gudorf accepts, is about love of God
and neighbor. But, she notes, "sex is perhaps one of the best
life arenas for demonstrating that self and other are not nat-
urally hostile. Their relationship is much more complex."[19]
Sometimes tending to ourselves helps us to love others better, more fully. Certainly encouraging people in the ways
that lead to dysfunction and addiction does not help them to
pursue healthy marital or sexual relationships with others.

Moreover, though, Gudorf's statement calls us to consider
what we believe to be the relationships among self, God, and
other. Augustine mostly thought that you couldn't love God
if you were loving self and other. Other notable Christian
thinkers contend that the Christian life is at its heart about
radical discipleship—the denial of self to love and serve
Christ in others. At the end of Matthew 25, Jesus shares a
parable of the judgment of the nations, proclaiming that on
that day the Son of Man will come and divide people into
sheep and goats, based on whether or not they served him
well. Those in the sheep group seem unaware of what marks
them as righteous and thus inquire, "Lord, when was it that

we saw you hungry and gave you food, or thirsty and gave you something to drink?" And the Son of Man responds, "Truly I tell you, just as you did it to one of the least of these who are members of my family, you did it to me."

When we care for others, we serve the Christ in them. When we deny our selves, we presumably have more to give. If I give you my coat, because you have none, I am serving Christ in you. But then I'm without a coat.

Pleasure, though, is not a zero-sum game. If I give someone pleasure, there's not necessarily less for me. Au contraire. And if I pursue some pleasure for myself, there's not less for others. This is what Gudorf is getting at: sexual partners can be actual partners, working together, mutually benefiting. Self and other are not always, by nature, hostile to each other. In fact, every now and again, the pleasure increases when it's mutual.

But I think it's also worth pointing out that attending to our own selves is important, too. Each of us was created in the image of God, and each of us has sacred worth. We don't gain worth simply through serving others. That's a good thing to do, but it's not what makes God love us and it's not what earns us a spot on this earth. There's something valuable about each of us, in and of ourselves. Tending to our own needs is a good and important thing, because we are creatures, beloved by God, created with bodies to care for and delight in.

The biblical story traditionally trotted out as a clear prohibition against self-stimulation features a man named Onan, who is called upon by law and duty to impregnate his late brother's wife (biblical marriage!). Instead, he has sex with her but at the final moment, "spills his semen on the ground." You might be wondering what this story has to do with solo sex, but back in the day, masturbation was also called "onanism," after that guy and his intentionally non-procreative sex act. Remember, if you will, that for most of history the only guaranteed non-procreative sex acts were masturbatory, because contraception was not overly reliable. So, the tradition has it, non-procreative sex—pleasure without consequence—is sinful.

In my read of the story, though (which you can find in Genesis 38:1–10), Onan's real sin is that he is shirking his duty to his sister-in-law, having sex with her (and presumably enjoying it) without fulfilling his obligation and actually doing injury to her. The practice of marrying your sister-in-law, or giving your dead brother an heir, was a means of providing economic security and protection to a woman who would otherwise be without support, set adrift in a society where women were pretty much only sustained through their relationships with men. Onan has sex with Tamar, but denies her the means to protect or sustain herself. Pursuing pleasure at a cost to another, especially a vulnerable other, is displeasing to the Lord. Shame on Onan.

As the story of Onan illustrates, sexual pleasure can be a sinful thing. Obviously. But the sin is usually more about a broken relationship, a harm done to self or other, than the nature of sexual pleasure in and of itself.

More than being "not always sinful," sexual pleasure is also a delightful part of being human, and it's important to affirm that. Perhaps even more important, though, is to note with Christine Gudorf that the love of self, God, and other

are not inherently opposed: we can honor God and honor
our bodies by attending to our desires with care; we can help
our future partners out by figuring out who we are and what
we like and long for. The pursuit of pleasure can be used
to mask other needs and, indeed, to debase ourselves. But
we need not be afraid to know and love our bodies, for they
are gifts from God, made for pleasure, made for connecting
us to the world and its people. Whatever your experience,
past or present, with self-stimulation, a future full of good
Christian sex requires coming to terms with the questions
posed by sexual pleasure, and an acceptance of oneself as
worthy and deserving of that pleasure, as a creature beloved
by God.

Chapter Two

Firsts

On the Whys and Wherefores of Desire

The girls in our sophomore English class were in agreement: this boy was hot. Tall, dimples when he smiled, *soccer player* (next to swimmers, known to have the best athlete bods), blond but unafraid to dye his hair on occasion, smelled like Cool Water (the cologne we, in our virginal states, referred to as a "do-me" scent).

After using my feminine wiles (i.e., reading a funny essay I'd written aloud in class) to capture his attention, I asked him to girls' choice. The following week, he asked me to the movies. It was all considered a bit of a coup. He was hot. I was most decidedly not.

Sophomore year only a few kids with December birthdays

drove, so dating in our suburban town mostly entailed phone calls and getting rides to the movies from parents. This meant that the boy and I spent little time outside of school in actual, unobserved proximity to each other. Tittering girl-friends always swarmed around at school; we had roughly four conversations that I can recall. One in which he handed me his headphones and played me the Sheryl Crow cover of "D'yer Mak'er," another in which we talked of the death of pets. He sent me a postcard from his spring break vacation. It was not love.

It was not love, but I was desperate for him to kiss me. Not necessarily because of some burning desire to be close to him, to know him—I was in fact terrified of such a thing—but because I was fifteen and had never been kissed. Not on the playground in grade school, not at church camp or the eighth-grade graduation dance, not by my Homecoming date. My destiny as an "old maid" was well on its way to being fulfilled, I was sure of it. Kissing a recognizably attractive boy would change all that.

We broke up a scant four months later, before he got around to kissing me, when my parents grounded me (for maybe the most rebellious thing of my adolescent life, leaving a church lock-in at midnight for donuts and a visit to a moonlit Lake Michigan beach nearby) for the rest of the summer. Before that infraction, it never occurred to me that I could or should be the one to make a move; I never imagined that he might be shy or insecure. In my adolescent despair (grounded all summer!?), I self-sacrificially set him free. At which point he immediately began dating my friend and became her first love. These things happen.

I was devastated, though it was probably clear even then that my motivations for being with him were of, shall we say, dubious moral worth. Luckily, only a kiss was at stake. For most of us sexual desire, and its relationship to sexual activity, is often pretty complicated. We may well have many reasons for wanting things, many reasons for taking action. Faithful people would probably prefer that our reasons for connecting with someone else sexually were to manifest the care and love and glory of God rather than a simple physical impulse. But how do we know what makes a desire good, life-giving, and holy? We are complex people, and our decisions and desires are subsequently equally complex.

Desire complicates the already theologically complex nature of pleasure, for if pleasure is a "premoral good," as we saw in the previous chapter, desire raises questions of morality. Is desire, wanting, always sinful, or does it depend on the object of our desire? What desires can rightly be pursued? When? With whom?

Here, I want to reflect on "firsts" to help us to understand our complicated desires. Throughout this chapter we'll explore the different facets of desire: Is desire ever sinful, or evil? What makes sexual desire a wonderful, holy thing? And what makes a desire—even an unmarried, sexual one—an opportunity for grace? We'll look at the ends of our desires, the call to self-reflection, and try to imagine how sexual desire might be "love trying to happen."

THE SOCCER PLAYER, as I mentioned, became the first love of one of my girlfriends, and I spent a couple of months mourning and moping. I recovered quickly enough, however, when my own first love arrived six months later in the form of another athlete, a boy who ran track with my best friend and made the whole class laugh. We had gone out in groups, to dinners and movies, and he asked me to Homecoming the night of a friend's birthday party at his house. After the dance he held my hand and I (brazen hussy, no longer leaving anything up to chance) kissed his cheek as I walked him to the car.

A week later I was home sick from a speech tournament (drama nerds for the win!), and my family was out for the evening. This young man called to ask if he could stop by. He brought me a box of Swiss Miss instant hot chocolate, to help me feel better, and some music: the first and, to most people's knowledge, only Hootie & the Blowfish CD, and a copy of REM's *Automatic for the People*. With any sort of distance from the moment, this combination of offerings would seem ridiculous, if not actually the opposite of romantic. But it was perfect. "Hold My Hand" was on the radio constantly and offered a fitting invitation; REM was his favorite band; and only communists hate hot chocolate.[1]

He rang my doorbell, came in, and presented his gifts. We made small talk before he hugged me, gave me a quick, closed-mouth kiss on the lips, and went home. I, being sixteen and only able to process my life through conversation, went back to my room to call my friend. This kiss, no disrespect to my young beau intended, was not the life-altering event I had imagined it would be.

I had expected to feel different: somehow more fully alive, or more connected; I had expected to be overwhelmed with romantic feeling. Maybe awakened from an enchanted sleep, or saved from a witch's curse. I expected that the first brush of another person's lips on mine would be charged, would feel different, truth be told, than if we'd just brushed arms. The musicals, Disney movies, and romance novels I'd been raised on may have raised expectations, but so had our night at the dance. He had held my hand, stroked my palm with his finger. An apparently absentminded gesture riveted my attention to this boy, made me lose track of time, caused me to blush and thrill. Surely given all this, and the fact that I really liked him—because this was not simply the result of a playground chase—this kiss would feel momentous.

Upstairs on the phone, my friend Erin prompted, "Well . . . ?"

"Is that all there is to it?"

She was nonchalant. Kissing isn't always all it's cracked up to be.

THE PREVIOUS SPRING, Erin and I had sat together in a state-mandated health class as we learned about drugs, eating disorders, and sexually transmitted disease through a combination of fiercely dry textbook readings and showings of ancient after-school specials. Teaching the course was the sophomore girls' basketball coach, and to say he was more uncomfortable with the subject matter than his students were would be a dramatic understatement. We passed notes full of our adolescent, but certainly amusing, commentary almost constantly through that class, but I give thanks for it: it's a too rare blessing (or too rarely respected right) for American teenagers to have access to comprehensive sex education these days.

My absolute most favorite part of that class was the typology of making out Coach presented us with.

"First, you've got your kissing. Then, French kissing. Light petting. After you start moving into heavy petting, you're getting awfully close to the Danger Zone."

He was certainly trying to tell us something important about taking things slow, and making sure we weren't getting in over our heads—teaching us what we needed to know in order to avoid accidentally passing some point of no return when unprotected sex was bound to transpire. To his credit, our trained and certified teacher did not resort to any sports analogies, especially regarding rounding the bases. But we just laughed and sang Kenny Loggins under our breath.

That night when my new boyfriend arrived to kiss me, this, then, was what surprised me. Our lips met, in my empty house! and yet afterward I was not one inch closer to the Danger Zone.

It only took a week until the boy and I had another go at the kissing thing. On this occasion, we patently ignored the Meg Ryan–Tim Robbins vehicle *I.Q.* for the duration of its hundred-minute running time. God bless his mother for clearing out of their living room, and for clearing her throat loudly as she came back in to make tea.

That's not a facetious comment: I felt blessed by the give and take, the intimacy and the excitement, of this first make-out session. The only danger involved lay in our desire to kiss until our previously untested lips grew chapped and puffy, but I learned something of deep importance that night, a lesson affirmed over and over during the months we were together: I could pursue my desire to be close to someone and feel good about that desire before, during, and after.

Now there are those who would dispute this conviction, and would wonder why my parents kept letting me leave the house when it was increasingly obvious that this boy and I were doing more than watching movies and drinking hot cocoa.

THE FIRST STORY of human desire offered by the Bible tells of a pursuit with long-ranging and widespread consequences: The Lord has prohibited the first man and woman from eating the fruit of the tree in the middle of the garden, but the woman sees that the fruit looks good, and she wants some. She acquiesces to her desire—whether it's hunger, curiosity, or some potent mix of motives—and eats. Subsequently, as the story goes, the happy couple is banished from the garden and cursed; the rest of humanity is likewise cursed—*original sinners* courtesy of these first parents. Human desire, it seems, brings nothing but trouble.

I have little kids now—three daughters—and my husband, Josh, and I routinely revisit the distinction between wants and needs with them: you are hungry and *need* something to eat; you *want* a Happy Meal or an ice cream. You *need* clothes that fit; you *want* that ridiculously overpriced shirt that resembles the one you saw on TV. Just because the distinction is easy for me to see, doesn't mean it's as clear to them. Also confusing is that sometimes—often, if we're lucky—our needs and desires can be simultaneously met. We can be hungry, need sustenance, and desire something healthy. Sometimes the warm, comfortable sweater we need is also beautiful. This is, actually, part of my goal in parenting: not just to help my girls to differentiate between needs and desires, but also to bring them into close alignment.

Certain strains of Christianity think that pursuing any sort of desire short of God is sinful, and that the most ascetic lifestyle possible is the holiest. Fasting, vows of poverty, lifelong celibacy: these aim to make room for the Spirit and conquer sin by shrinking the self, by diminishing or denying various needs and desires. Sometimes those practices can become dangerous, motivated by the hatred or distrust of our God-given bodies.

For these strains, both the objects of our desire and the act of desiring itself are problematic. Eve was guilty of two sins: wanting the forbidden fruit, and then eating it. That is, *I want the apple, so to hell with the prohibition against my having it. What I want is the most important thing.* Desire leads Eve astray, and it's been known to do the same for many of us. We might fairly wonder whether our desires—or the bodies in which they seem to have their origin—can be trusted. I wanted the soccer player to kiss me, so when he showed up at the church lock-in and my friends suggested we go for a spin after lights-out, I thought maybe the moonlit beach would be an encouraging venue. Desire clouded my judgment.

Later, after that seminal viewing of *I.Q.,* I learned that Coach was on to something in his description of the Danger Zone. For the first time, I experienced the pull of something that was both within me and outside myself, to *keep going—* that powerful feeling of not wanting something to stop, of not wanting to stop. In Romans 7, there's a passage that's often labeled "the inner conflict."

> For I know that nothing good dwells within me, that is, in my flesh. I can will what is right, but I cannot do it. For I do not do the good I want, but the evil I do not want is what I do. Now if I do what I do not want, it is no longer I that do it, but sin that dwells within me.
>
> (18–20)

My boyfriend's mother would always graciously clear her throat on entering the room, but I'm sure she routinely saw more than I would reasonably have wanted her to see as he and I lingered in an embrace for a moment too long, unwilling to stop. I didn't want her to see, but I didn't want to stop. So I didn't.

Desire is powerful.

But is it necessarily the sin that dwells within me? Is it evil to make out with someone you really like? Is that what Paul's getting at here?

Sebastian Moore, a Benedictine monk and theologian, offers another reading of the Genesis story that seems relevant: one that claims we're misunderstanding desire when we "equate it with egoism."[2]

Rather than the manifestation of selfishness and sin, desire, Moore contends, "is love trying to happen."[3] Does desire come from some lesser cosmic force, some lower part of our human architecture, from outside of us? Is it always and necessarily evil? No. Desire is about us figuring out who we are, and how we can be in relationship with others.

The desire for pleasure can, as we saw in the first chapter, be a perfectly healthy and holy thing: we need body pleasure. And, for me, the desire for and exploration of pleasure were part and parcel of coming to trust my boyfriend; they were part of falling in love. The desire was love trying to happen.

In the best of all possible worlds, it would ever be so. But, of course, that's not always the case. Moore concedes that "no desire is so prone to self-deception, to the very subtlest ploys of our egoism, as is sexual desire."[4]

During my sixteenth year, I am certain that my egoism was making more than subtle ploys, but at the same time I was—gratefully, ridiculously, with limited success at secrecy— learning about myself, about my desires, and about how to be in a relationship with another person, body and soul.

The experience of making out with this strawberry-blond boy, of being close to another body, moved me to awe and wonder, but it wasn't just the physical pleasure of it that kept me on that couch at his house every weekend for the better part of a year. As many people, women and men, young and old, know, if you're in the market for a quick peak or release of tension, you can take care of that physical urge with relative efficiency on your own. Sexual pleasure, and sexual desire, are about more than the sensations brought to you by the nervous system and the sensory responses that accompany blood flow to varied regions of one's body. The experience of good sex—and the delightful things that lead up to it—is one of risking showing and sharing oneself with another, of giving and receiving care and attention, of connection and delight. It tends to require a partner, and an enthusiastic, sensitive one as well.

For all the ambivalence of the Christian traditions toward desire, and sexual desire in particular, for all the warnings and prohibitions, our holy scriptures nonetheless contain a deeply erotic and romantic love poem in the Old Testament (Hebrew Bible) book called the Song of Songs (or, sometimes, the Song of Solomon). Perhaps because it's so erotic, faithful folks have a long history of trying to contain the passion, claiming it's clearly about marital love between a husband and wife, or an allegory about the love of God for Israel.

But, well.

In chapter five, the woman describes a fevered dream:

[Woman]
I was sleeping, but my heart was awake.
A sound! My love is knocking:

[Man]
"Open for me, my sister, my dearest,
    my dove, my perfect one!
My head is soaked with dew,
    my hair, with the night mists."

[Woman]
"I have taken off my tunic—
    why should I put it on again?
I have bathed my feet—
    why should I get them dirty?"

My love put his hand in through the latch hole,
    and my body ached for him.

> I rose; I went to open for my love,
>   and my hands dripped myrrh,
> my fingers, liquid myrrh,
>   over the handles of the lock.

(5:2–5, CEB)

Despite the millennia separating us from this text's ancient author, many of us may know that feeling: of hungering and longing for the touch, presence, taste, scent, sight, and even sound of the one we desire. The speaker pleads with her sisters, "If you find him, tell him this: I am faint with love."

Puffy lips, breath shallow, and rapid, flushed cheeks: Friday nights found me faint with love. It wasn't just the actual fulfillment of desire that led to such exquisite suffering; it was often simply, as the songwriter says, *the nearness of you*.[5]

SEXUAL DESIRE CAN be about a lot of different things: about feeling powerful, alive, about experiencing attention and pleasure. It can also open us to love and acceptance by daring us to risk knowing another and being known. It may sound crazy, but sexual desire can be a means of grace. That's why I don't buy that Song of Songs is mostly about Israel.

I recently read Rainbow Rowell's incredible young adult novel *Eleanor & Park*.[6] It's marvelous for all sorts of reasons—Rowell handles issues of gender, class, race, abuse, and love so perfectly—but the descriptions of her protagonists slowly falling in love, largely over the course of the daily ride to and from school on a hostile bus, struck me as so true. Maybe it's because I remember the thrill of sitting next to a beau, shoulders leaning in, hands entwined unless periodically stealing away to cup a knee. Eleanor and Park don't even share their first kiss until roughly halfway through the book, and yet the sexual tension and the desire they feel as they joyously discover their mutual interest leap off the page.

One of the things that makes *Eleanor & Park* work so well is that Eleanor narrates a chapter, and then Park does the next one; back and forth we go (much like the Song of Songs), seeing them each from their own perspective and then from that of their beloved. This narrative strategy captures the pathos and incredulity of these first-time paramours, but it also offers a powerful counterargument to those through-out history who fear that sexual desire and passion lead us inward—away from love of God and neighbor—who fear that attending to our desires and passions will make us selfish and hedonistic.

Eleanor loves the color of Park's skin, his voice, and his eyes. He loves her red, curly hair, and the sight of her figure—the one she thinks is too squat and curvy—makes him blush and dream. Part of falling in love is coming to see another person; part of falling in love is allowing another to see you.

But that seeing and being seen, and the vulnerability and attentiveness they require, are not just factors of a singular, committed, long-term love. Some Christians like to claim that all sexual intimacy outside of marriage will necessarily feel cheap and damaging, but many of us know that that's simply not true. The grace of being seen and known, of holy attentiveness to a partner, is possible, I'd argue, in any just and loving action toward another, and it's part of what makes sexual encounters—or good ones, anyway—so pleasurable.

Their desire is particular; it is not for just anyone, it is for *this man, this woman*. They only have eyes for each other.[7]

The desire to be seen and known, the desire met for Eleanor and Park and our biblical lovers, is not merely the stuff of literature and poetry. That desire is wrapped up in our very human need to be authentically ourselves and to be accepted as such.

Perhaps equally widespread among teenagers and young adults is a fear that we will never have this desire fulfilled. A good number of my survey respondents wondered at some point in their lives if they would find someone who would desire and appreciate them. Whether they were too skinny or too fat, too acne prone or shy, "one of the guys" or "not a guy's guy," they worried desperately they'd never be the object of anyone's desire.

I was certainly among those worriers for a number of years. I was convinced no one would ever see me as desirable, could ever possibly see beyond the giant glasses and crazy hair, the flat chest and the shyness. Teenagers tend to imagine that everyone is always focused on them, and particularly on their faults or vulnerabilities. They fear everyone is always talking about them, having judgmental opinions about their most personal attributes (what psychologists call "false audience consensus," the false belief that their behavior is the focus of others' concerns and attention). What's worse, no small number of tortured teenagers has asked over the ages whether it's better to go through life unnoticed, or to be seen for who you are, and judged.

I lived with the same question as that first real relationship began. When it became apparent that this boy was going to want to see and/or touch my barely-As sooner rather than later, I alternately panicked and dared to dream. It seemed as though that sort of touch would feel good . . . when we kissed I wanted nothing more than for him to pull me closer and caress me. But I was deathly afraid his hands would finally traverse my torso, only to recoil in shock and horror on realizing how empty the cup of my light blue Victoria's Secret bra really was. Is it better to be overlooked or known and deemed undesirable after all?

When the moment—the specifics of which are lost to history and memory—finally came, none of my fears were realized. Instead of being horrified by my body, he was delighted to be invited to access it. While I had feared rejection, that night and on many more that followed it, I felt appreciated and *altogether desirable,* not in spite of who I was, but because of it.

Theologian Paul Tillich once preached a sermon called "You Are Accepted!"[8] No matter how unacceptable—how deficient, or shame-filled, or faulty, or fallible—we feel sometimes, the fact of God is that we are accepted. Each and every one of us. In the life, death, and resurrection of Jesus as the Christ, we see that the estrangement we experience from God and one another and ourselves can be, even *is,* overcome. We're not separate from God; we're reconciled. We're accepted. "Acceptance" is late-1940s psychological jargon for grace.

There's a grace, then, in sexual intimacy that's mutually pleasurable. There's grace in deeming someone worthy

enough to see and know you; there's grace in being seen
by someone in a new way . . . and maybe even coming to
see yourself in a new way. There's grace—and passion and
delight—in coming to know another's scent, another's taste,
another's body; and to see oneself as having a particular, and
beloved, scent, taste, and body.

That grace is not merely something we *want*, though
there's nothing inherently wrong with desire; it's not just
about meeting a fundamental human need, though certainly
meeting fundamental human needs ought to be of critical
importance for Christians. Rowan Williams, the former
Archbishop of Canterbury, suggests that this grace, the
body's grace, is critical in helping us to understand the character and nature of the Triune God.

> Grace, for the Christian believer, is a transforma-
> tion that depends in large part on knowing your-
> self to be seen in a certain way: as significant,
> as wanted. The whole story of creation, incarna-
> tion, and our incorporation into the fellowship
> of Christ's body tells us that God desires us, *as if*
> *we were God,* as if we were that unconditional re-
> sponse to God's giving that God's self makes in the
> life of the Trinity. We are created so that we may
> be caught up in this, so that we may grow into the
> wholehearted love of God by learning that God
> loves us as God loves God.[9]

Three centuries earlier, John Wesley spoke of how
Christians might experience grace, and might help others

to experience grace. He did *not* list adolescent make-out sessions or sex of any sort as a means of grace. His list included things like regular participation in Holy Communion, daily study of the Bible, and working to serve the poor and imprisoned. But I like to think that if Wesley had lived just a few centuries later, he might have at least considered including kissing or teenage making out or sex, because he, like Williams, considered grace to be a powerful force for transformation, of individuals, society, and the world.

The means of grace Wesley described don't earn us salvation or teach us anything new or different about God. But they can be channels of grace, ways through which we experience God's love and life. So: never let it be said that taking Communion will save you, or that kissing your girlfriend will teach you something of God you cannot learn otherwise.[10] It's not the means themselves that make a difference; consuming bread and grape juice, even nicely prayed-over bread and grape juice, will not magically or suddenly change your life. But it can be a way of experiencing the presence and love of God, without which, in Wesley's words, the love of God waxes cold.[11] Visiting people in prison, caring for the poor, singing and worshipping in community, sharing a common meal: all of these can help us and help others to experience the transformative power of being seen and desired by God as significant and wanted. So, too, can sexual interaction be a way of experiencing grace.

UP UNTIL NOW, I've been hoping to get at what makes sexual desire a wonderful, even holy, experience by intentionally talking about sexual activity that is not as intimate as intercourse, but also pretty enjoyable. At this point, however, a turn to discussing "virginity" and what we tend to think of more broadly as "sex" can reveal the ways we are able to hold multiple types of desire in tandem and to consider if any of those types are more or less life-giving.

Over the course of that first romantic and sexual relationship, I experienced the grace of having affection lavished on me, of feeling significant to someone in a new way. I loved that boy because he was funny and smart, and had both charisma and these beautiful forearms. But I also loved him because of what he saw in me, someone smart and funny and lovely and desirable. Someone with no boobs to speak of, but with big blue eyes and clear skin.

My first love was my first in a number of categories; but he was also the first in a category that, at sixteen, I didn't know existed.

Once we'd been together for six or eight months, we had the opportunity to spend some time together without his mother in the next room. The promise of privacy, real actual privacy outside of a car, raised a question. Would we "have sex"?

For me, for us, that meant intercourse. Though I'd never describe my family or church culture as particularly concerned with virginity and its associated virtues, in the milieu of teen movies and health class in which I existed, sex meant heterosexual intercourse. As my first relationship deepened, as I had my own experiences of "will they or won't they," I grew increasingly irritated by the way TV shows and movies showed teen love and conversations about sex. Couples seemed forever to be asking questions of whether to "do it" or not after a few closed-mouth kisses and the placement of the boy's hand gingerly on the outside of her shirt. There was no natural progression! No sign that their sexual relationship was related to a shared intimacy, even when the couple was purportedly in love. No demonstration that if she wasn't comfortable with his hand in her bra, she was certainly not going to be comfortable with anything involving genitalia. Joey and Pacey should never have been talking about sex if they couldn't even manage to discuss second base.

There was also the sticky little problem in all those portrayals of young women uninterested in sexual pleasure; that was the guy's primary concern and pursuit, while she wanted love and affection. I love Carole King, but the progeny of "Will You Still Love Me Tomorrow" are myriad and unhelpful. Sexual activity of any sort in these narratives seemed transactional: What would she sacrifice of her purity in order to get affection and love?

I wouldn't continue to be so bothered by these scripts if they didn't play themselves out both in wide social surveys and in the much smaller survey I ran for this book. Many women had sex for the first time for love, or because their partner wanted it, or because they had made up their minds that they were old enough and ready—in a rite of passage sort of way—but not because they desired it for themselves. Not because their partner had awakened the desire to share this powerful experience of vulnerability and grace.

I worry about those who have sex too young, because sex renders you vulnerable; because the younger you are, the less likely you are to use protection; because the younger

you are, the less likely sex is to be a loving, mutually pleasurable thing, and the more likely it is that sex is a risk-seeking
behavior. But even more than age, I worry about those who
embark on sexual encounters or relationships devoid of any
real desire to do so; who become sexually active for reasons
other than desire for pleasure, grace, or intimacy.

Social scientists writing about people's self-reported reasons for having sex for the first time talk about the conflu-
ence of several factors: affection for their partner or an
expression of love, curiosity about sex, and desire for physical pleasure all constituted various motivations. So did peer
or partner pressure, or the influence of drugs or alcohol.
Then there are those whose first sex was forced. But there
are other, less nefarious, external influences: whether or
not the individual had a partner, or unsupervised time with
that partner—was there more than one parent living in the
home?—or was considered physically attractive by self and
others. Did the person have a vision of his or her future that
would be disrupted by pregnancy or disease? Did the individual have a religious belief system or family understanding that exerted "social control"—i.e., that suggested sexual
contact was to be avoided? Somewhere in the meeting of all
these factors lies the probability that someone will have sex.

When I asked my survey respondents why they had sex
for the first time, almost no one gave just one answer. There
was dispute about what constituted sex, and what those
first experiences ought to be called. "Loss of virginity" is
fraught, because "virgin" carries a host of differing connota-
tions and ascribed social values for women and men, and
because it implies a loss of innocence, or purity, while many

experience becoming sexually active as a gain—of pleasure, of connection.

For straight, suburban me, at sixteen and as I still understand my own story, virginity was about vaginal intercourse; for many others, though, it's defined differently. Most straight respondents to my survey calculated their number of partners the same way, and referred to their loss of virginity the same way I do. A smaller number of respondents included oral sex in their definitions. But a number of gay respondents suggested that their first sex occurred while giving or receiving oral sex, or simply touching each other's genitals, or even lying naked together exploring their partner. The decisive criteria for them was physical intimacy, not penetration. Many other LGBTQI respondents (and some straight ones) defined a sexual partner as someone present and involved in your achievement of an orgasm. (Hands go up from the crowd of straight women protesting that this criterion would shift their partner count dramatically.) A lot of people wholeheartedly rejected the use of the term "virginity" at all. (In some social science literature, this moment is referred to as "sexual debut," a phrase I sort of like, but which calls to mind some sort of strange debutante ball.)

A number of wonderful things were revealed in these responses to the survey, but the most critical to this conversation lies herein: sex is not easily defined; it defies boundaries and calls for interpretation and the assignation of meaning by those engaged in any given encounter. This is worth noting because having nurturing, good Christian sex is not about drawing lines in the sand: it is not about assigning different sexual acts to "bases" and forbidding some while permitting others. The overwhelming emphasis of certain segments of our culture, for example, on first, the importance of protecting one's virginity, and second, the utter normativity of heterosexual intercourse, has contributed to a surprisingly large percentage of teenagers who don't consider oral or anal sex to be "real" sex or challenges to their "virginity." And thus they engage in those things without understanding anything about vulnerability, mutuality, or the spread of sexually transmitted infections. That can't be what we're hoping for as we try to make sense of our experiences and guide others toward faithful practice.

Now, sixteen-year-old me couldn't have told you about the social construction of virginity, but it wasn't something I was overly hung up on. I rounded some bases more quickly than others, and when the question of "going all the way" arose, I looked around at my peer group and realized that I wouldn't be the first to cross the plate. One of my girlfriends had sat her parents down and given them the talk when she was ready to start sleeping with her boyfriend. Another had been raped. One "lost her virginity" while she had her period, and a tampon in, so there was great debate in our circle as to whether or not that actually counted. He had "put it in," but he couldn't have gotten very far.

I had never imagined waiting until I was married to have sex. Though the curriculum our congregation used suggested that sex was best in marriage, I knew faithful adults, people I admired, who had had sex before marriage. Also, I did not intend to marry immediately; I could not even begin to imagine getting married. I knew about various forms of birth control, and my mother had always told me that, when the time came, if I needed to come to her for help getting it, I could. (She did not imagine I would come seeking it in high school, however.) Sixteen seemed to me then as good an age as any; Brenda on *90210* was sixteen (even though all the actors on that show looked at least twenty-five). I loved this boy, and he loved me, and we knew how to make each other feel good—loved and appreciated and pleasured—both physically and emotionally. But when the moment came, I decided I wasn't ready after all. I wanted to . . . but didn't feel ready.

I just knew it in my gut. This wasn't the time.

Physical, sexual desire, it turns out, can be overcome.

Maybe it was because my mom had told me how much harder it is to end a relationship once you've had sex. Maybe it was because I was scared of the pain I anticipated. It wasn't fear of disease or pregnancy, because I attended a wonderful public high school with a mandated health class in the days of the Danger Zone and factual information about the effectiveness of condoms.

Whatever the reason, I changed my mind. And my first love respected that. We even dated a while longer and never really had the conversation again. I wasn't ready then; I wasn't ultimately ready for three more years, several "almost, but not quite" partners later.

By the end of our relationship I wasn't substantially more mature than I had been when he first showed up with Hootie and hot chocolate. But I had learned that sex wasn't just a rite of passage. However cute the soccer player from English class was, kissing him to get that first kiss over and done with, devoid of the actual desire to feel his lips on mine or to know him more deeply, wouldn't have felt right, any more than sleeping with this boy when something unidentifiable in my gut urged me not to would have.

IN RETROSPECT, I am so glad that I did not sleep with anyone in high school; those relationships were formative enough as is. But I think one of the reasons I waited (such as the waiting was) was because the choice was mine to make.

There are those who believe that our bodies and culture will always lie to us, but that God is clear about what is right in every circumstance regarding our sexuality.[12] In a culture that, today, seems far too often to suggest that women's and girls' bodies are for assaulting, I hear that. And as a once hormone-addled teen, I know that our desires ought not always be allowed to trounce on or ignore other voices within us. Again, as Christine Gudorf suggested, sexual pleasure is *a* good among many goods.

I remain unconvinced, however, that God is clear about what is right in every circumstance regarding our sexuality. We'll explore sexual ethics and varied ways of interpreting the Bible in the next chapter, but it should be obvious that "clear" is the last word that should be used to describe the intersection of our faith, the will of God, and our desires in context.

I give thanks and praise that I got to grow into sexual activity the way that I did, over time, with peers and partners who desired and cared for me, as I did them. Choosing what felt right and good, safe and exciting, wise and a little foolish, over and over again in each encounter taught me all the right lessons. They did not always stick. By the time I did "have sex" for the first time, I did it for a handful of reasons, only some of which were good. The boy was charismatic, but the relationship was shallow; we had a pretty impressive physical chemistry, but it was clear we lacked long-term compatibility. Very clear. Still, those sweaty Boston nights will get you . . .

We didn't really intend to sleep together, but then one night we argued at a party, and, well, made up. For the first time in all my years of making out, my body seemed to be craving that final step forward. My desire had always been sated prior to getting there; that night, I'm not sure. Between the heat and the alcohol and the reconciliation . . . I was a month shy of twenty. I think I thought I was ready. I think that I probably was. It felt amazing, which surprised me, but may well have had to do with the fact that my party attendance had rendered me very relaxed.

Unsurprisingly, once we consummated our summer fling, the shallowness of our relationship became evident in short order. I had some expectations, maybe, of how we'd talk about it. He, who had had a single prior partner, perhaps felt guilty for this inadvertent and certainly unpremeditated "deflowering." We never talked about it; we never talked again, not until a week before graduation, at the senior week clambake. Instead, my roommate walked me to the Planned Parenthood to get some advice, and then we road-tripped to Bar Harbor.

Desire is a complicated thing. Our bodies can encourage us to pursue things our reason might eschew, but this is an inner conflict. A divided self. Our desires come from within. Our bodies are not forever lying to us, are not evil-tending

entities to tamp down and contain until we can safely un-
leash them into the proper constraints of holy matrimony.
Our bodies *are* us. We are human creatures, which means
we are body and soul, made in the image of God, made
with bodies. The key profession of our faith is that God was
not against taking on a body, and so did! God came to live
among us in Jesus Christ (Philippians 2:6–8, among others).

Neither, then, is human life about protecting ourselves
and striving for security and certainty. That's certainly not
what Jesus did. Sebastian Moore locates our confusion about
the nature of suffering (for a long time believed to be deserved as punishment for indulging our desires) and desire
within the last part of Jesus's life. The theologian suggests
that Christians have too often interpreted the meaning of
the cross thusly: we suffer for following our desires, whereas
Jesus suffers not for following his desires, but for following
the will of God.[13] But that's all wrong, according to Moore.

> The truth is surely that Jesus does suffer for fol-
> lowing his desires. That is what the cross is all
> about. His desire, totally liberated toward union
> with God, totally resonant with God's will, draws
> upon him the vengeance of an unliberated and
> fearful world. And he draws us to follow him on
> this *via crucis,* this way of liberated desire in an
> unliberated world.[14]

Moore goes on to name those who are "sufferers for unde-
nied desires . . . who speak for the desires of the oppressed
millions . . . men and women who have dared to desire."

He's thinking of Gandhi and Mandela and King. But all of us, he continues, are called to this: not to deny our desires, but to attend to them, to ask what it is that we want from this life. In attending to our desires, we can separate out free will from compulsion. And, we hope, over time we can come to be so much a part of the life of God that our desires will be in line with those of the divine.

Taking up our cross to follow Jesus is not about living in fear of accidental pregnancy or even about protecting ourselves from heartbreak. When he exhorts his followers to take up that cross in the Gospel of Luke, Jesus tells them, "All who want to save their lives will lose them. But all who lose their lives because of me will save them" (Luke 9:24, CEB).

Jesus didn't come to live among humanity so that we could live our lives afraid of ourselves, our bodies, and others. Jesus came that we might have life—even pleasure—and have it abundantly (John 10:10).

In my high school boyfriend's den, I experienced desire as a means of grace; in my college apartment, it was considerably less holy, but an important experience nonetheless. The former was, I think, my introduction to a part of the abundant life I'd only read about: being seen and known, appreciated and valued, given pleasure and care. On that hot Boston summer night, I followed my desires to their natural end; I listened to my body. What I didn't manage was to listen to both my body and my mind together. That takes a little more practice. And, whether our "firsts" came when we were younger or older, for reasons good or bad, the work ahead lies in learning to recognize our desires and examining how they fit (or fail to fit) into a vision of the abundant life. How we rightly become like those who "dared to desire," how we pursue that life abundant in ways that are holy, and loving, and just; in ways that fulfill the commandment to love God, self, and neighbor, is the work of sexual ethics, which we turn to next.

Chapter Three

Playing Fair

The Ethics of Good Sex

I f sexual pleasure is a good, and God desires for us to live an abundant, joy-filled life in our divinely crafted bodies, what's to keep us from banging everyone we possibly can from the moment puberty starts to rear its ugly head?

I spent my freshman year of college single, having heeded the advice of countless teen movies and cast off the shackles of my last high school romance. Oh, sure, I made out with each of my high school boyfriends when they came to visit, but it wasn't serious. I was shy, and have never been the sort of person to successfully pick up partners at parties or bars.[1] The boys in my small academic program were all in relationships (many of which lasted past Thanksgiving!), and the wider university pool was terrifyingly huge. This year of undesired singleness was actually fantastic—I made friends I loved dearly, fell in love with Boston and academia, and found I had very little passion left for the roller coaster of late-adolescent dating.

By the next fall, though, I was ready for some companionship. As often happens at the beginning of a new school year, our circle of friends expanded. I hit it off with one of the new members. Our politics were just different enough that we flirtatiously sparred over ideologies; we liked similar music. We were both big-time nerds, who wanted to talk about course readings and papers we were writing. We went out on a single date, but it was weird. Like, super weird. He tried to hold my hand in the cab; I was embarrassed in the restaurant. I felt awkward in my skin, awkward with him. I liked him, but there wasn't that mysterious spark, that comforting electricity, I'd come to expect with boys I dated. I liked him enough to be friends, but not enough to date him, not enough to call him my boyfriend.

The problem—the sin—came a bit later. I knew after that disastrously awkward date that we were not going to be a couple, but at some point during an evening spent flirting with him at an alcohol-fueled gathering in our dorm, he kissed me. And I kissed him back.

My friends advised against this, when one or another of them encountered us in a clinch in the hallway near the bathroom. *You don't like him like that!*

I didn't like him like that, but I liked kissing him. There was a certain chemistry in our banter that got me charged up, and he was always willing. Week after week, we'd end up in some deserted hallway, or my room, getting as close as we could in the semi-privacy of communal living. He was tender, appreciative. I was respected and attended to, and when I was feeling lonely or lame or concupiscent,[2] I always had someone to make me feel pretty and desired.

But I didn't offer that assurance, that pleasure, in return. Oh, sure, I was as handsy as he was, a sexual agent as much as a recipient. But sexual sin is less about particular acts or the way they're carried out than the way partners treat each other; sexual sin is about a lack of mutuality, reciprocity, and love.

Our sexuality is a part of us—a part of who we are, something to be cherished and attended to, something for which we need never feel ashamed. Sexuality is a part of human life—the way we inhabit our bodies, the way we express ourselves, the way we grow into our relationships—and Christians are called upon to be reflective about the ways in which we live out our sexuality, just as we are called upon to be reflective on the rest of our identities and practices. In many ways, the same rules apply in the bedroom as anywhere else: love God, love your neighbor as yourself. Those are the sexual ethics—or, more simply, the principles that guide how we practice our sexuality—that we'll explore further in this chapter. Let's take a look at how Christians can faithfully engage the Bible as a source of those ethics, but also look to other sources for our norms—those baseline principles. These are age-old discussions, but we'll consider some contemporary language and thinkers, focusing on respect, autonomy, and consent as means of loving your neighbor.

The love of neighbor is a deceptively difficult thing, especially in regards to sexual relationships, because just as in the rest of our lives, sin prevents us from doing this fully, unambiguously. So, as we begin to examine Christian sexual ethics—the systems of just love and just sex—we have to start with sin.

WHEN IT COMES to sexuality and sin, the questions are many, and often loaded:

What counts as sexual sin?

Is it anything you wouldn't want to do in front of your parents or pastor?

Is it anything illegal?

Does it have something to do with consent? Or marriage?

There is certainly a strain of American Christianity that suggests that any sexual thought or contact outside of marriage is sinful. That God made sex for marriage, and thus (heterosexual) marriage is the only place in which that pleasure can be fully and rightly enjoyed in a way that honors God and the desire to honor God in your partner. Sin, in some definitions, is to counter biblical commandments and thus offend the will and holiness of God. Which is why some have taken verses from the Bible about sexuality and said that to live counter to them is to sin.

The definition of sin, however, has not been always and everywhere agreed upon. Biblical scholar Paula Fredriksen opens her book on sin with a discussion of just this. Even in the earliest years of the Jesus movement, as the canon of scripture was being set, even in the first several centuries of the church, there was an incredible diversity of views about what constituted the good life and what sorts of activity could or would keep you from it.[3]

The party line that dominates much Christian conversation around sexuality is that sex is best in marriage, or (in more progressive circles) marriage-like relationships. Much like definitions of sin, however, understandings of the nature of sexuality and marriage have not remained static over time, and those varied understandings have had an ambiguous legacy.[4]

When it comes to living out our sexuality, finding a sexual ethic that helps order our lives and relationships, while being flexible enough to respond to a variety of unforeseen situations, seems more important to this Christian leader than simply trying to get people to be able to repeat the rules of their community's moral code. Sure, we can insist that one remain a "virgin" until marriage, for example, but what does "virginity" entail? As we saw in chapter two, the word means different things to different people. Sexual intimacy is not easily classified or parsed into distinct categories.

In the last chapter, I suggested that the Christian life is less about protecting ourselves from being profaned and more about learning to risk ourselves in love. This is a developmental task as well: as human beings grow and rely less and less on their parents' protection, they must learn to navigate the risks of increasing involvement in the world.

But if so much of our understanding of morality is shifting and changing, if Christians in particular want to draw lines of holiness in new places, we need to spend some time articulating what, in fact, it might mean for us to "play fair" or engage in "just love" or even "sacred sex." If the norm isn't going to be "don't have sex until you're married to someone of the opposite sex," what is going to replace it?

THE FIRST STEP toward answering all those questions is to explore how it is that we know whether something is good or bad, right or wrong. What sources of authority or wisdom can Christians look to?

Maybe it's too obvious to say that we can, and should, look to the Bible. That's what I did in the first chapters (Genesis, Song of Songs) and in this one (Romans, Matthew) and in most subsequent ones as well. There's a good deal of diversity in how Christians interpret the Bible and understand its authority, but just about everybody believes it's of critical importance for Christian life. The Protestant tradition I am a part of, so-called mainline Protestantism, has some ways of talking about the Bible that are like a lot of other Christian churches, but unlike others. For example, mainline Christians tend not to talk about the infallibility of scripture. We don't say it's the inerrant Word of God. We talk more about the divine inspiration of its human authors. We talk about it as a record of God's relationship with humanity, about its continuing influence on and power in our lives, and about its depths and breadths. We talk about the Bible as the Word of God, but acknowledge that God continues to speak through the presence and work of the Spirit.[5]

That seems like a simple enough statement once it's broken down, but there's one more complicating factor: the Bible has a whole mess of human authors, who wrote over a period of hundreds of years, and these diverse folks sometimes had different interpretations of similar topics.[6] Finally, the Bible was written a really long time ago, in societies that were vastly different from ours. Its great age is no reason to discount the biblical witness—I tend rather to think the fact that this ancient text continues to speak to the heart of little old twenty-first-century North American me is pretty miraculous—but I mention it because there are things we know or understand differently now.

The Bible is such a rich resource—a treasure trove of insight and poetry, of inspiration and critique. Because of its richness, its complexity, it calls to Christians of many stripes to take it seriously, refusing to oversimplify its meanings or to proof-text[7] to get the answers we want to see. It's a complicated resource for reflection on sexuality, in particular, but there's no way around it: Christians have to engage the biblical text in constructing our ethics.

When Christians are trying to figure out what a sexual ethic might look like, then, it's important to place the Bible in conversation with other sources. The most reputable ones among Christians tend to be reason or knowledge, tradition or collected wisdom, and experience, both personal and of others.

In other words: *What makes sense? What has the church said over time? What about theologians or philosophers or secular academic disciplines? What's true to my experience, or that of my community, or my friends?* Christians can locate their ethical norms within the intersection of all these sources, though even in the intersection there can be varying interpretations. Christian ethics are tricky—but we hope that with these varied sources, and a commitment to scripture, we can find enough that holds us together while also leaving room for difference and the change the Spirit often brings.

AFTER CONSIDERING WHAT sources Christians might rightly use in the work of determining sexual ethics, we can turn to the content of those norms. Indeed, some might wonder at this point why we need sexual ethics in the first place. If there's no such thing as "normal," why bother with "norms"?

For Christians, there's a pretty simple answer: sin.

Now, sin as I understand it is not about breaking rules or offending God's delicate sensibilities, but is rather that force within us and in our communities and world that pulls us to do, as Paul puts it so beautifully in Romans, "the evil I do not want." Instead of always being smart and kind, of doing what is in our own best interest or the caring or respectful thing toward others, we do something stupid, or callous, or cruel. We do things, all of us, that evidence how far apart we sometimes feel—and sometimes are!—from what God hopes for us and for the world. Sin hurts people, and thus it's important to name it, stop it, and work for healing and justice.

Some sin is obvious to name: sexual exploitation and abuse. Some types of sin are harder to see: passively allowing the vulnerable to be abused, turning a blind eye or a hard heart toward those who are suffering, or denying one's own complicity in systems of injustice. A few years ago, a report came out about the failure of a number of U.S. universities to support their students who have been victims of sexual assault. Those administrators aren't raping anyone, but they're not exactly free from sin when they shrug their shoulders and suggest that the perpetrators don't need punishment or consequences for their violent acts.

Sometimes, though, sin is banal: the kind of thing that gains somebody a reputation as being a jerk, but would never be brought up in a court of law. Sin isn't always, or usually, criminal, after all. This sin is the sort that manifests our failure to love our neighbors as ourselves, and to love God with all our heart, mind, soul, and strength. It's the kind of sin that stays with you long after you've stopped committing it, that drags you into moments of self-loathing and regret.

I didn't realize at the time that when I was fooling around with my college friend, I was actually sinning. This would come to mind as I later read twentieth-century Jewish philosopher Martin Buber.

Buber argued in his most famous work, *I and Thou*, that human life is structured around two different word-pairs, "I-It" and "I-Thou," which is to say that we have two ways of being in the world. The first is the way we experience objects, things, the world. It's a one-way relationship, in which the individual subject "I" experiences or uses things: trees, the breeze, a ball, a spoon. The latter is a relationship, in which there are two subjects, two people, who can never fully or really "experience" or "use" or "know" the totality of each other, but can only be in living (moving, changing) relationship.[8]

One of the groundbreaking things about Buber's work was the way he described God as the "Eternal Thou." God is not an object—a fixed thing—that we can grasp, or use, or explain completely. Rather we are in relationship with a living God. That's an important insight to bear in mind when Christians or other religious leaders start wagging fingers about the clear and knowable will of God. When Moses demands to know the name of God before venturing off to liberate the enslaved Israelites, the Lord answers that the closest approximation of a name might be "YHWH," four Hebrew letters we tend to transliterate into English as "Yahweh" or "Jehovah," but which really make an odd statement: "I am who I am" (Exodus 3:13–14). God will not be pinned down. The only way we can know God is through an ongoing relationship, through the revelation of God's presence and self over time.

Christians can see the truth of this insight reflected in the prelude to the Gospel of John.

> No one has ever seen God.
> It is God the only Son,
> who is close to the Father's heart,
> who has made God known.

(JOHN 1:18)

No one has ever seen God, but Jesus, the Word, makes God known to us. How does this Word become known to us? In one sermon? In one list of commandments? In one healing? Nope. The totality of God is known only through the fullness of a life, from birth to death (and on to resurrection and eternity).

Like any good philosopher, Buber is concerned not merely with questions of metaphysics, but also with those of ethics.

What does this "I-Thou" business have to do with late adolescent make-outs of questionable prudence? If God is the
"Eternal Thou," all our partners, parents, neighbors are regular, everyday "Thous" to whom we are related in innumer-
able varied ways.[9]

If I use a spoon to eat my cereal and then cast it aside on
the counter when I no longer need it, there's no harm no
foul. A spoon is made to be used. An earnest young poli-sci
major, however, is not.[10]

When another earnest young poli-sci major, back in
Jesus's day, approached the great Teacher, he asked, "What
must I do to gain eternal life?" What's good? What's good
enough to put me in the company of God forever?

Jesus, in that lovely Jesus way he has, answers the question with a question: *What's written in the law? How do you
interpret it?*

> "You must love the Lord your God with all your
> heart, with all your being, with all your strength,
> and with all your mind, and love your neighbor as
> yourself."
>
> (LUKE 10:25–27, CEB)

In Matthew's Gospel, Jesus is asked point-blank the greatest of the commandments, and he says the same thing.[11]

> He replied, "You must love the Lord your God with
> all your heart, with all your being, and with all
> your mind. This is the first and greatest command-
> ment. And the second is like it: You must love your

neighbor as you love yourself. All the Law and the
Prophets depend on these two commands."

(MATTHEW 22:37–40)

Loving God, the Eternal Thou, requires all our heart, all
our being, all our mind. Loving our neighbors—Samaritans,
girls next door, boys down the hall—requires that we value
and understand them as we would ourselves: as subjects, as
actors and agents; people, complicated, living people, just
like us.

There's a third part of that, too: we're commanded to
love ourselves. If earnest poli-sci majors deserve to have the
sanctity of their lives as created by God recognized by others, so do all of us. If my friend-to-whom-I-was-a-lousy-friend
had any sin in our ongoing relationship it was in not loving
himself enough to quit putting up with my nonsense and
poor behavior.

In this way, in this Jesus-said-we-should-do-it-this-way approach, Christian sexual ethics are like any other Christian
ethics. This ethic arises out of a singular norm: love the Lord
your God, and your neighbor as yourself.

SHOULD OUR SEXUAL ethics be more complicated than that? Or
more specific? We can read Martin Buber all we want, but
what should it look like practically in our lives? One of my
survey respondents, a religious woman who is still unmarried in her thirties but has had several sexual relationships,
wonders if there's something she's missing in her attempts
to order her sex life by the precepts that order the rest of
her life. She grew up in a church culture that very much

suggested that sex was for marriage and marriage alone, and
that homosexuality was not condoned by God, but as she's
grown in faith, and as she's seen what I'd call the "varieties
of human experience," she's not convinced those convictions
reflect the will and intent of God.

But she also wonders if in leaving those convictions behind, she's developing an anything-goes practice that allows
her to do what she wants without feeling guilty, instead of an
ethic that challenges her to live as a faithful disciple.

A college student in a group I spoke with recently made a
wonderful observation: So much of Christian talk about sexuality focuses on what acts are okay—can unmarried people
hold hands? Kiss? Share a bed? Touch each other? Bring
each other to orgasm? Engage in varied acts of stimulation
or penetration? One survey respondent, a young lesbian,
heard routinely that heterosexual intercourse was off-limits
for the unmarried, but didn't know how to set boundaries for
her own romantic relationships. Given that she was always
with women, there was no temptation to engage in "penis-
in-vagina" sex or "p-i-v" sex (as the kids are calling it these
days). Did that mean, she wondered, that she was free to
add anything else she pleased to her sexual repertoire? (She
doubted it, but used the example to point out the limitations
of sexual moralities that focus exclusively on "virginity.")

Different communities have different understandings of
what constitutes sexual morality, and as Christians, many
of ours have had quite a lot to do with marriage and love.
Imagine, if you will, a Venn diagram with circles for love,
sex, and marriage. Those three things are each complex
in and of themselves, as hugely important parts of human

experience, and in relation to one another. But too often, people conflate them in various ways, collapsing each into a single type of experience with only one just or holy purpose.

When Christians speak now of why marriage is the best and proper (and only) context for godly sex, there are good arguments to be made, but it is worth noting that Christians have not said the same thing about sex and marriage since the days when the biblical writers first took stylus to papyrus. Neither does the Bible offer a consistent or systematic approach to the subject matter. As ethicist Margaret Farley writes, we find rather "only occasional responses to particular questions in particular situations," and "a serious exegetical and interpretive task" should we want to glean answers to our questions about what is right and good and loving.[12] Which is to say: it's not a good idea to proof-text with the Bible, especially around love, marriage, and sexuality.

These days, when Christians speak of marriage as the context for sex, when they claim that "God created sex for marriage," they may mean several things: that sex can lead to the conception of children, who require years of care and tons of material resources most easily provided by a stable couple; that the commitment of marriage can help us to let go of our fears and to feel safe in the emotional and physical vulnerability that sexual relations entail. Monogamy between healthy partners is the best way to avoid contracting sexually transmitted diseases. There's something wonderful about sex in the context of covenant love.

All our sources of collected wisdom, however, suggest that simply because sex exists within marriage does not make it holy or just or loving. Spouses are perfectly capable

marriage is not a sufficient norm

of treating each other badly, and even, in some situations, abusively. Marriage, to use the language of ethics, is not a sufficient norm. It is not a sufficient condition for just love or just sex.

A woman I know, Annie, got married when she was just out of college, to the Christian boyfriend with whom she'd crossed her own boundaries for premarital intimacy but had not had intercourse. He intimated before their wedding that now that she'd compromised her virtue with him, she was no longer pure and they were bound together, if for no other reason than that no one else would ever want what he had already had. They married, and he was verbally and emotionally abusive. She left him within a few years, which infuriated her in-laws and took all her courage, but was absolutely necessary for her health. After the divorce, she began dating an old friend, and in the course of that relationship, they had sex. It was fun, loving, and pleasurable, and though they ultimately broke up, she was glad she had slept with him. "For me, it reclaimed sex, after it had been something harmful in my marriage. It was good to be reminded of what sex is supposed to be like."

What is sex supposed to be like? What are the conditions that make for "just sex"?

Margaret Farley, whom I cited above, published *Just Love: A Framework for Christian Sexual Ethics* in 2006, as a culminating work near the end of her time on the ethics faculty at Yale Divinity School. A member of the Mercy Sisters, an order of Roman Catholic women, Farley became a bestselling writer on Christian sexual ethics when the Vatican issued a statement in 2012 criticizing the book for a host of "general problems," as well as its deviation from Catholic theology on questions of, among other things, homosexuality and masturbation.[13]

After the statement came out, you couldn't get a copy of Farley's book on Amazon. It sold out. And rightly. *Just Love* is brilliant, and faithful; it also offers two important insights to our discussion here: an imagining of what constitutes just love and/or sex, and an exploration of what sources Christians can rightly use in reaching ethical decisions.

Farley cites the good work of a number of ethicists, and suggests that their criteria are all well and good, but wants to make justice an underlying principle for both love and sex. A just love, she argues, will have certain characteristics, regardless of the type of love relationship, and just sex ought to manifest them, too:

1. "Respect for the autonomy and relationality that characterize persons as ends in themselves, and hence respect for their well-being": *Poli-sci majors are neither toys nor spoons, and must not be treated as such, even if they did just try to argue that Reagan had an effective tax policy.*

2. "Respect for autonomy": *Partners have to be able to give consent, and give it freely and enthusiastically.*

3. "Respect for relationality": *Are we in this together as equal partners? Are we committed to this relationship in some way, and to playing fair within its boundaries? Is this relationship obnoxious or is it adding some good to the world?*

4. "Respect for persons as sexual beings in society": *Does this interaction reflect the freedoms and affirmations we want all people to have? What does this hookup add to conversations about and understandings of social justice?*[14]

Maybe these seem too obvious; maybe "love your neighbor" seems a given. I'm surprised, though, by how often I find the insistence on consent and autonomy questioned in Christian circles. Melanie Springer Mock has noticed it, too, and said as much in her brilliant article for *her.meneutics,* the women's blog of *Christianity Today,* written for a primarily evangelical audience:

> We may assume that Christian teaching on sex and sexuality inures us from having such discussions about affirmative consent: because abstinence education teaches young people to avoid situations where consent might be needed; because Christian youth will not be incapacitated by substances that often complicate questions about consent; and because talking about "yes means yes" promotes sexual activity outside of marriage. (Never mind that that affirmative consent needs to occur within marriage as well.)[15]

Springer Mock writes as a mother of adolescent boys, but also as a professor who teaches undergrads, keenly aware of the national scourge of sexual assault on campuses and beyond. She knows that community norms for premarital abstinence do not guarantee abstinence, or a lack of nonconsensual sex. She continues:

Helping young people understand affirmative consent might be difficult given Christian teaching about abstinence, but such conversations are imperative. Fundamentally, the Christian faith relies on outdoing each other in showing honor (Rom. 12:10), and on loving one another as Christ loved us (John 13:34). Affirmative consent challenges us to honor the worth of each person. Nonconsensual activity challenges this notion, suggesting that a person is worthy as an object for our own pleasure. Surely we can see the problems in this kind of coercion, whether it happens within or outside the bounds of marriage.[16]

Some Christians write about consent as if it is not a necessary conversation, as if Christian faith somehow cancels out the need to know and ensure, in each and every encounter, that it is mutually desired. Or, more frequently, we hear that an ethic of consent is insufficient. Insufficient to capture the fullness of freedom in Christ and God's plan for sexuality,[17] insufficient to prevent rape.[18] Conor Friedersdorf, writing at *The Atlantic*, suggests that "individual consent has replaced all other moral considerations," as if that's a bad thing. In Farley's work, consent is only one of several baseline ethical norms, but none of the others work without it. Friedersdorf, having dismissed the usefulness of an ethic of consent, goes on to propose something else: What if Christians reminded people of Jesus's call to "be good to one another" and suggested that they apply that call to their sexual lives? Consent isn't enough to meet that standard. Say, he muses, there's a girl you like and she'd like you to kiss her and you'd like to kiss her, but she's had a bit to drink and you know that you don't actually like her all that much, and that kissing her might be leading her on. "Be good to her." Don't kiss her.

Say, Friedersdorf muses again, you are dating someone with whom you would like to have sex. She enthusiastically consents. But you feel, somehow, that she is not ready for the emotional import of sex. Best to hold off. "Be good to her."[19]

On its surface, there is much to recommend Friedersdorf's approach. Erring on the side of caution is generally good advice, though not one likely to be heeded by college students. (I'm not throwing shade, either. There are times in one's life during which one is more likely to privilege caution. The time when one is eighteen to twenty-four is not one of them.) But what irks me, other than the denigrating of the value of consent, is that his suggestion does not take seriously what your desired partner is telling you. It's paternalistic, and it errs on the side of assuming you know what is best for someone else. That does not meet Farley's criteria for respecting another's autonomy, nor even those offered by Springer Mock. It does not honor a person to assume you know them better than they know themselves.

Consent, autonomy—this is tricky business, and we can often be blind to the complexity of navigating relationships in ways that are holy and life-giving instead of sinful. Loving others, though, requires paying attention to our own motives, and regularly checking in with a partner—current or potential—about their needs, hopes, desires.

Growing up, I'd read the Bible and I could have told you about the Sermon on the Mount, and the "greatest commandment," and I probably held those teachings of Jesus at the center of my faith and ethics, such as they were. But as an undergrad, I generally thought the Bible's most relevant contemporary application was around poverty policy.

That ongoing bias (coupled, to be fair, with the obliviousness of youth) was just one of the things that blinded me to how poorly I was treating my college friend, and, awesomely, contributed to my ridiculous hypocrisy. This boy and I would debate welfare policy and I'd cite that commandment and the commitment to neighbor love, and then I'd go upstairs and treat him like, well, not much like a good neighbor.

I didn't see that I was hurting him, that while we were both consenting, all the other norms of mutuality and respecting his full personhood and particularity were being neglected. I told him casually about other boys I liked; he was not my boyfriend, I did not think it would bother him. I assumed he liked other people and was simply messing around with me while he bided his time waiting for something else to come along. Alas, I was projecting.

I'm still not convinced varying levels of physical intimacy are rendered appropriate and holy only within the bounds of marriage, but when we both returned after summer vacation, and I nonchalantly mentioned that I'd fallen in love, I saw in his crestfallen face, from my perch on our dorm washing machine, the consequence of my sin. He wrote me an impassioned letter, far more than I deserved, hoping that my new beau fully appreciated me—with my freckles and political passion. I finally realized that something can be more demeaning than messing around in a college basement hallway. I'd never worried much about how letting a boy touch me under my clothes compromised my virtue; it didn't even occur to me that mistreating a friend, or anyone, was a greater threat.

Farley muses that her insistence on justice might be perceived as stripping the joy from love and the fun from sex,[20] but that insistence on justice is so critical, not simply for keeping things consensual and legal, but because it is so, so easy to close our eyes to the ways we objectify others, to the ways we put our own needs and desires first, to the ways we fail to consider the feelings of others. Playing fair, engaging in just and ethical, but no less hot, make-outs, requires paying attention to the complexity of human relationships, needs, and desires. It would almost be easier to have a simple list of dos and don'ts . . . but think of all the mutual, creative, committed, and relational fun we'd miss out on.

Chapter Four

Singleness, Sex, and Waiting

Theology for the Search

I chose to attend college where I did based on a number of factors—how lovely the campus was, how easily accessible city life was. They gave me financial aid and offered so many awesome classes. I did not go with any anticipation that I would receive my "MRS."

As I headed toward the halfway point of my college career, though, it did begin to dawn on me that I did not want to be single when I graduated. I didn't need to marry right away, but I wanted to be in a relationship with a future.

That summer I met someone.

Our first kiss was sloppy and disastrous, such that I came home and cried to my roommates over my disappointment.

They counseled me to try again. They were right.

We dated for just over two years. He continued to be so smart and so funny and kind. Generous and hardworking and sweet. He was tall and lanky and though I probably outweighed him, I felt delicate in his arms. While I was a Christian, and actually started occasionally attending worship again while we were together, he was a Hindu (though mostly nonpracticing—a Diwali/Holi Hindu, if you will). We nonetheless shared a vision of what is good and true in this life. We valued family and travel, adventure and trust, poetry and math. We wanted to make the world a better place. We were awesome together, so very much in love.

I thought I would marry him. This is how things went: you meet in college, you stay together for a long while, and eventually, when you're old enough, you get married. We talked about it, that we would marry someday. My parents adored him. They didn't even seem to mind too much when they figured out we were sleeping together. That's how much they liked him.

Then I went to grad school and he stayed in Boston and we broke up. I was unmoored, lost. It wasn't just that I mourned the relationship, which I did, but I was afraid I wouldn't meet anyone, ever. I was afraid I'd missed my shot.

The Church Universal, as I hope is becoming clear, can be so entirely goofy on topics of sex, love, and relationships. Sex is a critical part of identity (but only if you are straight, and fit traditional gender roles, and are married). Singleness is great and easy to bear and a virtue, and celibacy is expected; but whoa, man, does God want you to get married and enjoy the marital bed (which is both joy and obligation!) and start cranking out some Christian babies who will complete your life and give you purpose. God will bless you with all these things (unless He chooses not to, in which case you are to submit to His will, too bad, so sad).

My tone here is ever-so-slightly biting, but for those whose lives have not included healthy, lifelong, heterosexual relationships that produce healthy biological children, even the unintentional exclusion offered by the church in its valorization of certain relationship types stings. Badly.

It's interesting that this is where Christianity has landed in the twenty-first century, given the church's clear preference for celibacy and singleness for much of its history: religious vocations to the priesthood or convent were far more worthwhile spiritually than marriage or caring for children; Paul invited folks to get married, but only if they couldn't be chaste like all the best people. How interesting that we're talking so much about married sex, when Jesus—the one whom we are called to emulate and follow—was likely not married and whose sexuality remains lost to history.

The church is not the only goofy one, of course. American culture seems to tell young adults, particularly young women, that they ought not settle down until their dreams are well on their way to being fulfilled, until their careers are fully launched, until they are ready for the ~~burden~~ responsibility of a committed relationship. They're supposed to experiment, but not too much; work hard and play hard; not get too attached, sow some oats, but be ready to marry by the time they hit thirty. The messages are clearly mixed, and they're not really helping anyone.

What do we want—out of sex, out of love, for our lives? What do we want and how do we attain it? Are we to sit back and wait for God to reveal our soul mate? Are we to marry at all costs? Must we remain celibate (if we were celibate in the first place) if we don't marry and adulthood continues its inexorable advance? Is there such a thing as a righteous, sexually active, single adult?

In this chapter we take up these questions and wonder a bit about how God is involved in our dating lives (or lack thereof). We'll also consider Jesus as a role model for single adults—one who challenged most of the assumptions about how adult men were supposed to settle down. Singleness can be a drag or a vocation or something else entirely; regardless, God calls us to be agents in our own lives while also providing comfort when things do not go according to plan.

A WOMAN I know recently began the New Year naming her grief over a broken engagement and her hope that this would be the year that God would bring her a husband.

Another friend of mine, in recapping her year, posted to Facebook a picture of a skeleton looking out a window. "Still looking for someone to marry," she captioned it.

One of my dearest friends just turned forty, and she has gone through several long periods of singleness: some intentional, time given for self-reflection and cultivating other relationships; others not so much. Another long-single friend has made it clear that she is open to being set up by friends; *play matchmaker,* she invites. Two men I know spent their twenties dating casually, actively refusing to settle down, only to get a little panicky in their thirties, on realizing that they were each actually interested in being married and becoming fathers. One joined several dating services, while the other started mining his extended social circle.

A smaller percentage of people get married today than at any other point in U.S. history,[1] though that's sort of a misleading statement. Marriage has become an economic marker in a lot of ways; people with less economic stability just move in together and don't bother with the marriage. But it is true that remaining single is a more viable, socially acceptable option, too. Marriage and parenthood used to be seen as clear markers of the transition to adulthood; now you can stay single and still be a grown-up (though it seems to help judgy relatives come to terms with this if you manage a certain degree of success in your career).

What seems to make people happy—partnered or single—is feeling as though they have not been ill treated by God or the fates; what makes us happy is getting to choose, having a hand in our destiny.

There are those—plenty of those—whose sense of God is as the Divine Father of us all, who hears our prayers and answers them individually, in ways befitting the Divine Will, according to His time and His pleasure and His wisdom. This is a helpful way to think of God for many people, though it begins to grate on those for whom life is not going as they had hoped. Why has God not seen fit to send me a partner? What did I do wrong?

I confess, I'm not convinced that's how God works in the world.

ERICA, A PASTOR and close friend of mine, whose theology is more steeped in the work of John Calvin, a reformation theologian deeply committed to the notion of God's providence and sovereignty, jokes that "luck" ought to be a dirty word for Christians. It ascribes power to some force other than God. To give thanks for "good luck" is to ignore God's graceful action in the world.

She's probably right. Still, I'm reluctant to use words that traditionally describe the work of God to tell love stories. For reasons that have something to do with the complexity of circumstance, and the mysterious ways in which God works, we live in an unjust world, a world in which things don't always work out, for reasons good and bad. When we come face-to-face with what Paul Tillich calls "the riddle of inequality," what role do we suppose God takes?

A God in control of every contingency is not really a God you can praise with any ease when circumstance is often a terrible thing. I loved my college boyfriend dearly. We shared all the things that would have made for a wonderful life together. But we were young. And our graduate work led us to different cities. And our families lived around the globe from each other. And we weren't, ultimately, ready to change cities to be together for the time being. We were willing to try our hand at a long-distance relationship, but with no definite end in sight—*we'll be apart for two years and then marry and move together,* for example—things imploded pretty quickly (thanks mostly to my immaturity and inability to articulate my needs; he was lovely, always).

Things did not go according to plan, and we were heartbroken.

Sometimes the heartbreak comes earlier; in never-materializing opportunities for connection. In loneliness and isolation.

Some straight men work in industries dominated by men; they work all the time, and don't have time to build a community in which they might meet someone. Some queer folks live in places that are hostile to LGBTQI inclusion and suffer for their isolation. Some women live in New York City, where, it has been scientifically proven, there are no eligible men.

Circumstance, bad luck, ingrained sexism in the tech industry, and pervasive homophobia in the rural Bible Belt: these are neither the work of God nor things within our control.

Circumstance can indeed be wonderful: a few years after my college boyfriend and I broke up, I met Josh, a New York native, in Chicago, where he lived with his childhood best friend, Adam, who had met my high school best friend, Erin, at the University of Pennsylvania. When I moved back to Chicago for grad school, Erin thought I should look up Adam, now a student at the same university. There are so many relationships and decisions—so many beyond our control, so many that had nothing to do with us—that led to our meeting. And, eventually, to our being single at the same time, and sharing a lengthy conversation at that summer party in the Woodlawn Avenue apartment that preceded our first date a few nights later.

Maybe my hesitancy around terminology, though, can yet be remedied. Maybe I trust in providence and prevenience, God at work, if not a singular divine Plan. The eternal God may know and see me, but I'm pretty confident that the benevolent creator wasn't pulling the strings of a research biologist's career in order to get me a husband, even a very good husband.

THE NOTION OF a matchmaker god, attractive though it may be, miscategorizes the work of God and misunderstands the way humans are called to respond to that work.

In a world before radar or germ theory, genetics or an understanding of female reproductive systems, a god who directly intervened in human existence did not seem so improbable. The world was full of an abundance of happenings that defied explanation and it often made sense to attribute them to God or other divine forces. Things grew significantly more complicated for Christians in our scientific age. We still believe in God, and we see no particular conflicts between science and religion, but we need to think through what it means when we say "God is at work in the world."

Some Christians are comfortable with the idea of a god who exists and acts much like we do: whose ways are "mysterious" but who nonetheless "knows what's best for us" and acts to bring it about, either in creating a perfect mate for each and every one of us, or in designing each of our days and the unfolding of our lives as we meet and marry that mate. That god, however powerful and sovereign, feels supernatural, and a bit ambivalent. A god who lives outside the world, watching, stepping in when our prayers get loud enough or we make a big enough mess.

That god, I'll be honest, reminds me of Lord Business, the villain in the recent (and surprisingly fabulous) release *The Lego Movie*. Lord Business believes that everything belongs in a particular place; everything must be built in a particular way. Everything must be properly ordered and assembled, and if it's not, he'll resort to sinister ends to maintain that order. While I don't think anyone really believes in a fascist (or Lego) god, or one who (spoiler alert) deals in Krazy Glue, it's worth noting that a god whose plan trumps those of everyone else is not really the Christian God. The Lord invites Abraham to go to a new place, encourages Moses to return to Egypt and speak on behalf of the divine. Jesus calls people to follow him, to join him in serving.

God does not force our hands, or tap a divine foot impatiently while sulkily waiting for us to get with the program. We're cocreators with God; we're no longer slaves but friends. We're invited to choose.

In *The Lego Movie*, the heroes are "master builders," individuals who can pull together pieces from a host of different projects or even realms and create something wholly new and wholly useful. Theirs is an ability to envision something no one else would have imagined, and then to bring that vision to birth. I want to be a master builder when I grow up.

It may be totally ridiculous, but I think of God as something more like the inspiration that moves the master builders than the Man with the Plan. The creative energy that drives us in life, that thrives in diversity and freedom: that's God.

I get a bit persnickety about the claims we make about who God is and what God does. When we talk, for example, about an all-knowing, all-powerful god who lives way off somewhere who makes us each a perfect mate and waits until the appointed time to show up and introduce us to him or her at church,[2] it should make us wonder why that god didn't bother to show up to stop the violence in Syria, smite the guys who poisoned all those black kids with lead-filled water in Michigan, or cure that young mother's cancer. Or, perhaps more mundanely, why that god didn't send my friend a partner before she aged out of fertility, when she so longed to carry a pregnancy.

That's what theologians call "the problem of evil" and my former student Leah calls "the failure of a model of re-demptive suffering." Often pop theology suggests that God lets us suffer or struggle so that we can learn or grow. But I'm pretty sure I don't buy that. I don't think God would be willing to let anyone, much less make anyone, suffer or die so that someone else can learn some life lessons. That's not what Christians mean by "costly grace." Harkening back to chapter three, you'll recall that we are called to treat friends and partners as "Thous," as subjects with agency and sacred worth, not objects to deal with as we please. Surely, then, the God who loves all people equally and without bound is able to live up to the standard set for screwy little beasties like us. Surely God is not a jerk.

God doesn't treat people badly. Neither does God hold out on us. God wants to bring the world into what process theologians[3] call harmony and "intensity of feeling."[4] And yet, the "riddle of inequality" persists. Some people seem to catch more breaks than others. Some find the loves of their lives. Some don't. That undeniable unfairness *should* rightly bother us. And it should make us question our understand-ing of the character of God. How can God be loving and just and in control of everything, while doling out ble_____ __ some people and not others? I, for one, am not interested in a god who plays favorites.

If other Christians are also uninterested in that partisan god, there are two practices we must give up, particularly in our roles as well-intentioned/passive-aggressive friends, parents, and pastors: first, ignoring the grief, and second, fueling the shame that accompanies life in a culture that idolizes romantic love, married heterosexuality, and the nuclear family. There is a legitimate grief that accompanies the death of our expectations for our lives—the passing away of a vision for our lives that isn't coming to be. We're getting better as a culture at understanding certain other types of grief—grieving children never born, for example, or a hoped-for identity as a parent. But we still expect our singles to be sassy and fabulous and endlessly optimistic, even as relationships end, or doors seem to close; people need the space to grieve dreams deferred and to imagine new ways of being in the world, to carve out new identities.

The single hardest thing for long-single friends and survey respondents alike to bear—among those who were single but wished to be partnered—is the loneliness. Longing to be seen and known, longing for the grace-full experience of sexual and romantic intimacy and having that longing go unfulfilled. Singles aren't dying for a romantic Valentine's Day, but for a partner with whom they can comfortably ignore the made-up holiday.

Piling on the weight of loneliness is the burden of shame, often exacerbated by (sometimes well-meaning) others. *What is wrong with me that no one loves me in this way?*

Well . . . it could be that you're too focused on your career, or you don't work out, or you're too political, or . . .

What is hard is not knowing what you should be doing differently. What is infuriating is knowing that you're doing everything "right" and you're still alone. The Christian tradition doesn't really resolve the problem of evil, or even of loneliness and the injustice of unintentional singleness. But it does suggest that there's good news that's more powerful than sin and death, so certainly more potent than despair. That gospel lies in this: The world and its possibilities for goodness are nearly infinite; far bigger than we can imagine. There is enough love to go around. And we participate in it. We are individuals, with selves, located somewhere in the space between matter and memory, and we are holy and good, even if we haven't found a mate. We are complete, inasmuch as anything is complete. We can imagine creative ways to engage the contingencies of our universe and the vagaries of American coupling. Writer Tanzila Ahmed is wise: "I might not have a life witness, yet. But, at least, I do have a contingency plan in place. And maybe all the witness that I need in my life is simply my own."[5]

IT ISN'T FAIR that some folks remain single when they'd rather be partnered. Loneliness and longing can be artistically rich—"But Not for Me" is one of Ira Gershwin's finest; "Chasing Pavements" is one of Adele's—but usually that transformation, from suffering to beauty, or meaning, can happen only if we attempt to live into this one wild life we've been given, to look for possibility, to open ourselves to God's creative presence.

I'm pretty sure this is the call on our lives from no less than Jesus, the world's most famous single person.

Now, I don't mean to burden single folks with an impossible standard of forever resisting temptation and remaining pure in thought and deed. Rather, I embrace the notion that Jesus was fully human and fully divine. If he was fully human, he experienced all the joys, pains, and ambiguities of living in a body, of going through puberty and experiencing the rush of hormones, of being a sexual creature who longed to be in relationships of various sorts with other people. Human.

I get really, unreasonably, irritated by suggestions that Jesus was married and the church tried to cover it up, or that Jesus was gay and the church tried to cover it up. Basically I get irritated by conspiracy theories. I find compelling, instead, scholar Dale Martin's argument in *Sex and the Single Savior*, namely that "Jesus has been a figure of ambiguous sexuality."[6]

Martin examines a number of different interpretive strategies (or imaginations, as he calls them) Christians have used to reflect upon Jesus's sexuality. He argues that we really have no way of knowing for certain what Jesus's sex life (or lack thereof) was like. The church fathers definitely thought he was celibate, but we don't know for sure. Some historians note that Jesus may well have been married, because just about everyone married in Nazareth in that day and age, and the fact that no spouse is ever named suggests that it was so ordinary as to not warrant mention.

Some scholars suggest Jesus might have been gay— there's all this business about the beloved disciple; there is the erotic homo-sociality of his relationships with the disciples.

I'm compelled by the idea that Jesus was probably celibate, but that it would have been for a purpose, and that it might have been hard to bear sometimes. We get a sense of his frustration, resignation, and loneliness on occasion ("remove this cup"; "the son of man has nowhere to lay his head"), but also the full, abundant life he modeled and preached. He was fully in relationship with many; he had intimate friendships, and he was dedicated to his work. If his celibacy was hard, he was not overly anxious about it; he leaned into the other parts of his life.

Martin suggests that Jesus's sexuality was ambiguous—we don't know—but that regardless of what his sexual practice looked like, he was kind of "queer." Queer because he didn't follow societal scripts, queer because he hung with women and men, queer because he was maybe celibate but not an ascetic, queer because he didn't marry as far as we know. Jesus was different.

Jesus was different and his path was likely puzzling to those around him, even as it puzzles us still today.

Can single Christians find hope in this, courage and sustenance here? As fully human, fully sexual, fully incarnate beings, who just happen not to be with anybody, single Christians can yet do good, saving work in the world. Singles can yet have intimate relationships. No one need be defined by relationship status or remake themselves to fit into existing social structures and roles. We can be like Jesus. Maybe celibate, maybe not. It's really no one's business but ours and God's.

I'M RELATIVELY CONVINCED, in an academic sense, that Jesus was probably celibate. If that gives hope to those singles trying to remain celibate, that's a great thing. If celibacy starts to stand in the way of abundant life for singles, they can rightly let it go.

Part of figuring out how to live into the creative life of God is figuring out how to live into being yourself, and choosing the spiritual practices and disciplines that support your own discipleship. One of the most unfair things the Christian tradition has foisted on singles is the expectation that they would remain celibate—that is, refraining from sexual relationships. American Christians sometimes conflate celibacy and chastity, too, which is a problem. Chastity is a virtue, related to temperance—it's about moderating our indulgences and exercising restraint. We're all called to exercise chastity in a variety of ways, though the details will vary given our individual situations.

In the official teaching of the Catholic Church, however, chastity requires restraining oneself from indulging in sexual relationships outside of the "appropriate" bounds (and bonds) of marriage. That is, chastity for singles means celibacy—no sex.

But as we've spent some of these first chapters considering, there might be other norms for chastity. Maybe our marital state isn't the primary norm. I'd argue that we can be chaste—faithful—in unmarried sexual relationships if we exercise restraint: if we refrain from having sex that isn't mutually pleasurable and affirming, that doesn't respect the autonomy and sacred worth of ourselves and our partners.

There are those who feel that they are called to seasons of

celibacy, or even years of celibacy, and if answering that call is life-giving and purposeful, then they should take it up as a spiritual discipline. But no call can be forced on an unwilling person, especially not if they find themselves single only by virtue of circumstance.

Plenty of women and men love sex, and need it—*we need bodily pleasure,* remember—and the abundant life for them will involve seeking out relationships of mutual pleasure. Chastity, or just sex, requires that whether we are married or unmarried, our sex lives restrain our egos in ways that destroy mutuality, restrain our desire for physical pleasure when pursuing it would bring harm to self or other.

I offer the example of Jesus not because I think he was likely celibate, but rather because his life demonstrates what it might mean to be both different and beloved, chaste but never cut off. Jesus was forever referring to those who have eyes to see, and he saw people in ways that others didn't. He saw them through the eyes of love, whoever they were. He loved them as they were, regardless of what society thought of them. We're called to see that way, too: to see and nurture the possibilities for life and love that are constantly unfolding all around us. We're called to see ourselves this way: beloved, no matter (or perhaps because of) our refusal to conform to society's expectations about sex, love, and relationships.

Straight, gay, bi, trans, intersex: we are beloved, and do God and ourselves a disservice if we are conformed.

Conforming is not the same as adapting, of course. If we are lonely and not partnered, we can create other kinds of families, networks of choice and caring. But this is not changing who we are, tamping down our God-given selves; this is creating something new, beautiful, holy.

Like the master builders, who look at the pieces before them and see past the instruction manual's designs toward something creative and unique, single and partnered Christians alike need to shut off the voices that proclaim that "everything is awesome" if our lives are just like everybody else's, if we are following the rules.

Our call is to discern where God is calling to us, what energy is pulling us, what doors are opening in our lives, and when that pull and those doors and those voices are most holy and good. When they speak to the highest truths about ourselves. When we're in relationships, or looking for them, that discernment has to be mutual.

ONE OF MY oldest friends and I once compared our "numbers"—the number of sexual partners we'd had. My number was substantially lower than hers. *Do you think I'm a slut?*

No.

She is still single. I have been with the same person for thirteen years. Even if she slept with only one person a year during that whole time—in relationships she thought had a future, in relationships in which she felt cared for—her number would be more than three times mine.

It's not for me to judge how singles navigate their sexuality beyond marriage. I got lucky, found someone I wanted to marry who wanted to marry me, even though I wasn't perfect, even though I wasn't a virgin. I got lucky: I made more good choices than bad, listened as best I could to the Spirit's leading, and was in the right place at the right time.

Another friend was single for a long time and finally decided he was ready to date with intention. But he kept blowing first dates. He had built up his expectations for each woman he actually worked up the courage to meet to such an extent that he couldn't maintain the casual fun of getting to know someone. He probably could have used some therapy. Instead he joined Tinder. It sort of worked the same way. He met a lot of different people—not all of whom he slept with—and the realization that there are, indeed, a lot of fish in the sea relieved some of the pressure to find "the One." And, not too long after, he found the One. Not on Tinder, though. On Match.com.

The God we know in Christ is the creative, loving force that moves in us, connecting us to one another and calling us beyond ourselves; the presence that calls us beloved—single or otherwise—and inspires us to joy-filled, abundant lives. We are both bound by destiny and free to choose our own paths. Things rarely go the way we have planned or have expected, but God is present, making all things new.

My friend Sandhya insisted that I listen to the David Gray song "This Year's Love," on repeat, while I wrote this chapter. It speaks of both hope and desperation, the longing for this relationship to—finally—be the one that lasts.

It's exhausting waiting on one's own. It's exhausting to seek the mystery of connection over and over. To offer oneself in vulnerability to the mysteries of love.

What attracts an individual to another? Why do we feel a spark with someone and not another, and what moves that attraction to action? The thing that moves you from dinner dates to a dynamic duo is a kind of intangible mix of pheromones and shared passions and compatible work schedules and a randomly shared but undeniable hatred of Lenny Kravitz's music. I've sometimes wondered if Josh and I would have fallen so hard so fast if it hadn't been summer vacation and we hadn't had the time to give ourselves over to the work of getting to know each other and being carried away by our enjoyment of this new romance. Would I have missed out on a life with him if I'd tried to date him while taking a full course load?

I don't know how to differentiate between idle thinking and probing the holy mysteries of connection; I suspect there is no clear difference.

There is always possibility, and then, in most things, there is decision. Decision never ends the story: our lives are comprised of the endless unfolding of decisions and possibilities. That's Gray's longing. This decision, this love: may it last and last. Whether it does or not, though, we continue to navigate the challenges of destiny and freedom, of shame and grief, of hope and vulnerability.

Chapter Five

Naked

A Theology of Vulnerability

I have this recurring nightmare. I've ended up at school, or work, or church, without any clothes on. I've apparently assumed a little casual public nudity is no big deal, only to realize far from my locker, office, or closet that this was a terrible idea. I am naked, and I am embarrassed.

I am ashamed, too—because my dream self is convinced that there is something crazy, something presumptive, something *wrong* with being naked, with showing oneself to others, with sharing oneself. This is a common enough nightmare, I know, which perhaps suggests that the need to come to terms with our nakedness, our vulnerability, in a variety of forms is universal. The Book of Genesis is not

great for a lot of things (history, geography, gender relations), but its first chapters reveal some important commitments about these universal questions. What does it mean to
be naked? Take Genesis 2:25:

> And the man and his wife were both naked, and
> were not ashamed.

That's the second Creation story in the book of Genesis:
in this version, a human is created first, and then, realizing
that it shouldn't be alone, God puts it to sleep and makes a
second one out of the rib of the first. They awaken, and the
first declares his delight in the second. In becoming two,
they become male and female: differentiated only in that
there are now two instead of one. Not primary and secondary, not hunter and gatherer, not leader and subordinate;
that is, not opposites. Just two selves, differentiated.

They're naked—having only recently been made of
dust and bones, after all—and they're not embarrassed.
Theologically, that point, made in the last verse of the second chapter of Genesis, has been pretty important throughout history. Christians have asked that verse to carry our
sense of humanity's innocence before the Fall (when Adam
and Eve, prompted by the devilish serpent, eat what God
has forbidden them to eat and subsequently get kicked out of
Eden). They were innocent, without sin, one with God and
one with each other and comfortable with themselves. Then,
they ate, and they knew that they were naked, and they
were ashamed.

Whether their shame comes from the realization of their

nakedness, or their creaturely status (as is suggested in chapter one), or from the regret of disobedience, the story goes that Adam and Eve ate that forbidden fruit, and then up and made themselves some clothes.

I wonder if part of their realization was that their nakedness is fraught. Sometimes nudity is glorious—like sleeping naked on a summer night, like sleeping naked on a summer night next to someone you love—and sometimes it's mundane. Sometimes it renders undeniable our vulnerability. Sometimes nakedness is dangerous.

Nakedness has been considered a vulnerability throughout history, from the time Adam and Eve first noticed it in themselves. But physical nakedness is just one aspect of our vulnerability; we are vulnerable creatures, able to be harmed emotionally, spiritually, and sexually. Would that we were so lucky as Achilles—whose tragic weakness was easily located (and, you'd think, might have been easily protected!).

We'll spend this chapter exploring the topic of vulnerability, and why appropriate vulnerability is necessary for experiencing just sex. Most of us have to spend a little more time reflecting on the ways in which we are individually vulnerable and where we have pockets of confidence, resilience, and ease. Knowing ourselves can help us then to establish relationships of mutual vulnerability and sharing. Letting our guard down, letting others see and know us, is a necessary first step in experiencing the grace of intimacy, but we want to do what we can to protect ourselves from undue harm as well. For a long time, marriage has been imagined to provide all the safety we need, but that is not always the case. Long before the intimacies of marriage, however, our understanding of bodies and nakedness is formed, usually first in our family of origin. So let's start there.

I GREW UP in a house of girls: two sisters, and a mother who owned the second edition of *Our Bodies, Ourselves*. Over the years, my sisters and I bathed together, we shared clothes, we shared a bathroom. We were all swimmers. We grew accustomed, from a young age, to being naked around certain people. I was infinitely more comfortable around my sisters, much younger than me, than around the other girls in gym class. I had a four-year lead time on my middle sister, and so even though I was a late bloomer, I wasn't embarrassed by the slight differences in our figures. In my sisters, I could see what my body had been; in my mother, I could see where my body would go. There were bodies at different stages, bodies that needed to be cleaned and dressed and cared for, and sometimes expedience necessitated nudity.

The varsity swimmers—among whom some of my closest friends were numbered—were totally in command of their nudity. After practice, they stripped off their suits, and washed their hair and stood around topless, talking and singing "Wonderwall" by Oasis. They dressed quickly but casually, motivated by the ever-approaching first-period warning bell, but not by shame. They inhabited their bodies with confidence.

I, flat-chested, hid behind a towel, but in an inattentive, sisterly environment, I grew in comfort. A body is a body. Mine was different in some ways, and I longed for a rack of any substance, but I was not ashamed.

Adam and Eve, our metaphorical parents, were not initially ashamed. In a marriage (though I've always been sort of bothered by the fact that she goes from "woman" to "wife" in the span of four verses), one hopes that there can be nakedness without shame or embarrassment. But they are not even embarrassed in front of God—and not simply "the [abstract] spirit of God in all things," but the Lord who walks in the garden with them and talks to them.

When you're a kid, you don't mind being naked in front of your parents, or, often, anyone else. At age four both my kid sister and my middle daughter believed one's birthday suit to be the perfect ensemble for running around the block, or reclining on the patio paging through a few picture books, or riding one's scooter around the living room. Kids only slowly begin to realize that their bodies are their own, and moreover, that others' bodies are separate from their own. They only slowly begin to desire or appreciate privacy, and learn to respect it even more gradually. (My kid, for example, wants privacy while she uses the bathroom, but doesn't mind barging in to talk to me while I'm going.)

Adam and Eve, innocent and blissfully unaware of the existence of Good and Evil, are like children. They aren't embarrassed, because they have nothing to hide. They aren't, as far as they can tell, separate from God in any meaningful way. They don't even know that's a possibility. So, in many ways, being naked is not a good or a bad thing, but just a thing we happen to be underneath our clothes. They are innocent, in those early days, but I'm not sure I'd describe their relationship as intimate, despite the fact that they are husband and wife, despite the fact that they are naked.

In fact, their relationship can't be "intimate," as we tend to think of it, because intimacy is defined not as the collapsing of two selves, but as the relationship between two who are distinct from each other. Until she eats before him, there's not a sense that they're ever not totally in sync, with each other and with God.

In the days of our own, actual, innocence, there's an easy camaraderie in everybody, boys and girls, getting stripped down and hosed off after an afternoon playing in the sand. Still, I wouldn't trade the delights of intimate adult relationships for it, even if the potential for intimacy also brings the potential for pain or embarrassment. Innocence is nice, but it's not somewhere I'd want to live.

The existence of sin—of everyone's capacity and inclination to do ill—renders us afraid of showing ourselves to one another. The context of our nudity, of our vulnerability, makes a difference. Some contexts, some relationships, some people, are safer than others; some reflect the joy of being "free and easy" (as my daughter and I describe nudity), while some are terrifying, and fail to affirm our integrity or the image of God in us.

How do we know which is which?

THE JEWISH AND Christian traditions writ large can be read generously (and why not?) as exploring and prescribing the circumstances in which our nakedness and vulnerability can be respected, appreciated, and honored. In the Bible, we see a good deal of division of the sexes: around menstruation, and worship. In Orthodox Judaism and Christianity, that continues to this day, though in some instances, it is

argued that that segregation was a doubling-down response
to external pressures that came with modernity. Still, the
creation and maintenance of what Naomi Seidman calls "homosocial" spaces, basically single-sex social arenas like the
Korean spa or the church women's retreat, sustains the possibility of that gracious (even erotic) same-sex awareness of
bodies that happens in some swim locker rooms. Seidman, a
Jewish academic raised Orthodox in Brooklyn, suggests that

> eroticism is produced, or permitted, by the ab-
> sence of members of the opposite sex, allowing
> for physical, emotional, and religious intimacies
> and connections forbidden in mixed groups—the
> shared ecstatic song and dance, common meals,
> and worship that is the peculiar genius of religious
> or traditional societies.[1]

The half-naked singing of Oasis.

There's something special about those homosocial set-
tings. But many of us also long for sexual relationships as
well, whether we're straight, gay, or otherwise. And we
rightly want those relationships to be safe places for the vulnerability of sexual companionship and (sometimes) for the
caring of children. If we're going to share our bodies with
someone, and/or make new bodies, we should feel safe to
share ourselves freely and without shame. The promise of
commitment and permanence in marriage helps to render
that relationship safe.

That's why many Christian churches and communities place such a high importance on marriage, and on sex

happening within the confines of marriage. Many adopt in theory a slogan used by the United Methodist Church: "Celibacy in singleness, fidelity in marriage." Those are the prescribed modes of appropriate sexuality for the two possible contexts in which faithful people might find themselves—single or married. It is believed, in theory anyway, that if we experience sex only within the safe, respectful boundaries of marriage, that we will be able to have a healthy, loving sex life with our partner. And, indeed, the implicit promise is that if we reserve sex for marriage alone, the sex will necessarily be effortlessly and immediately mind-blowing. That the sharing of oneself will come easily and painlessly.

No small number of evangelical Christians have been blogging against this mythical reward for celibacy or "purity." Mindy Spradlin joins the throngs listing the "lies I learned about sex growing up in church culture":

> Our wedding night and honeymoon were sweet and special and awkward and frustrating. We were in no way prepared for the fact that true sexual intimacy would take work and education. . . . Where was our reward? Where were the fireworks? Awkwardness turned into frustration which turned into shame which turned into bitterness which turned into a great divide.[2]

Raised to believe that not only sex but also desire and arousal were not supposed to be part of unmarried life, Spradlin learned to deny her sexuality and "turn it off."

On marrying, what was wrong would be made right, and she would be able to embrace her sexual side with passion, power, and excitement. But the reality, she laments, is that shame and guilt and inhibition do not, cannot, simply melt away.

Even in a marriage, nakedness and vulnerability are not necessarily without complication, just as sexual relationships outside the constraints of marriage—before it, or before it's on the table, or among widows and widowers unable to jeopardize their economic well-being for a walk down the aisle—are not necessarily dangerous or shame-filled.

The book *Real Marriage: The Truth About Sex, Friendship, and Life Together* is hugely problematic but provides a good example of how marriage does not guarantee a healthy vulnerability or uninhibited physical intimacy. Written by controversial pastor Mark Driscoll and his wife, Grace, it pushes every single one of my theological buttons. Still, despite Driscoll's failings as a pastoral leader, the opening chapter is revealing, and even helpful.

In *Real Marriage,* husband and wife chronicle the earliest years of their dating and then marital relationship. They meet in high school, both sexually experienced. She's a pastor's daughter living out some stereotypes; he's a bit of a ladies' man. At some point in college, he becomes a Christian, and shortly thereafter, God tells Mark to marry Grace. Simple as that.

They get married, and despite intentional and Christ-centered premarital counseling, things are pretty terrible. They had been "fornicating" before marriage, and though they'd stopped before their engagement and marriage, Mark had looked forward to "pick[ing] up where [they'd] left off sexually."[3]

> But God's way was a total bummer. My previously free and fun girlfriend was suddenly my frigid and fearful wife. She did not undress in front of me, required the lights to be off on the rare occasions we were intimate, checked out during sex, and experienced a lot of physical discomfort because she was tense.

Eventually, he has a vision in which he sees her cheating on him shortly after they began dating in high school. He confronts her with this, she confesses, and things go to hell. He wouldn't have married her if he'd known. She is so full of shame and self-loathing she can barely stand herself. But she's also bitter. He's bitter. They're married, they're monogamous. She's pregnant! But they're lonely and miserable, and clearly hard up.

After being married for more than a decade, and having four more children, she reveals an experience of sexual assault, and something changes. His heart breaks,[4] and he realizes that he was "so overbearing and boorish, so angry and harsh, that I had not been the kind of husband whom she could trust and confide in with the most painful and shameful parts of her past."[5] Grace, for her part, experiences God's grace urging her to let go of her fear and bitterness.

All this is not to say that marriage is terrible and marital sex is worse. But I offer their story because it serves as an example of how "commitment" or "monogamy" or even "marriage" is not the sole condition, or guarantee, of a healthy vulnerability or uninhibited physical intimacy in relationships. There's something additional going on, something worth exploring for those who want to know what might constitute "appropriate vulnerability" for singles. Karen Lebacqz, a theological ethicist, takes up the question in helpful ways, accepting the traditional notion that sex is "a gift from God to be used within the confines of God's purposes,"[6] but expands those purposes beyond procreation and union. She writes:

> Sexuality has to do with vulnerability. Eros, the desire for another, the passion that accompanies the wish for sexual expression, makes one vulnerable. It creates possibilities for great joy but also for great suffering. To desire another, to feel passion, is to be vulnerable, capable of being wounded.[7]

Without vulnerability, she continues, without openness, there's no possibility of union. But it's not just the threat of missing out on procreation and union that makes vulnerability so important. "Sex, passion and eros are antidotes to the human sin of wanting to be in control or to have power over another. 'Appropriate vulnerability' may describe the basic intention for human life."[8]

Looking back to Adam and Eve, Lebacqz suggests that the Fall is a sign of humanity's attempt to eschew our vulnerability; instead of union or intimacy, we see the hardening of hearts. Jesus, in turn, "shows us the way to redemption by choosing not power but vulnerability and relationship."[9]

"Whoever tries to preserve their life will lose it, but whoever loses their life will preserve it." That's the version from Luke 17:33 (CEB), but the Gospel writers have Jesus sharing similar sentiments elsewhere.

WE'RE CALLED TO take a risk. Part of being human is putting ourselves "out there," engaging in life and love and the world of other people. Being intimate, being naked, are big risks, and ones that are worth taking with people we trust to "play fair."

Not all risk-taking is good and holy, however. Jesus may go to the cross, but we are also called to love ourselves, to see ourselves as the dwelling place of the Holy Spirit and worthy of love and care as God's own beloved creation. Not all vulnerability is "appropriate."

There are the clear circumstances, like rape, which "violates the vulnerability of the one raped, but also . . . the rapist guards his own power and refuses to be vulnerable."[10] The norm here is a mutual vulnerability, a norm that can be missed in seduction, promiscuity, prostitution, or even in suggesting that sex is nothing more than a physical act.

Our culture has a hard enough time knowing when rape is rape, unfortunately, so knowing how to navigate relationships and encounters that actually fall into some blurry gray areas is an even more daunting task. Most human stories are more complicated than they first appear, and vulnerability can't always be seen. In the locker room, some of the girls I thought were so confident I later learned struggled with bulimia.

Other complicating factors include the way we conflate a

desire for privacy in certain situations with feeling shame. Or imagine that nudity is the same as immodesty. Or even that various stages of undress are directly related to similar levels of vulnerability. Just because we'd prefer to limit those who see every crack and crevice, every fold and bulge and line, doesn't necessarily mean we're ashamed of our bodies, though it may indicate that we understand that being seen and known opens us up to others. It's right and good that we should want to pick the people and contexts in which we're physically vulnerable.

Similarly, showering after gym, or wearing a bathing suit at the beach, or leaving the bathroom wrapped in a towel, is not necessarily immodest. In many religious cultures, including Christianity, people associate modesty exclusively with women, and their need to be forever covered so as not to excite the lusts of the men around them (who are, the argument goes, totally in the thrall of their vision and its ties to their basest instincts). Modesty is about protecting women from men, and men from unintentional seduction.

That definition irks me to no end. Moderation is good; protection of the vulnerable is good. But fundamentalists of many stripes use modesty as a means of social control, it seems to me, and apply it in ways that are far from egalitarian. Seidman tells of the Orthodox school she attended in her youth, and the thrill of same-sex celebrations of Shabbat. It was so appealing because, for one, the young women could sing the prayers aloud: "To sing aloud was not something we took for granted: a woman's voice was immodest, not to be displayed before men to whom we were not related . . ."[11]

Synagogue architecture traditionally separates women and men, ostensibly for this reason:

> ... to separate the spiritual from the sexual realm. Women, in this justification, represent sexual temptation to men—the sexual temptation men present for women is deemed irrelevant, as witnessed by the fact that men may not look at women but women are encouraged to look at men during synagogue services.[12]

Here, as elsewhere, women's bodies are less than men's. Here, women are literally silenced for their inherent immodesty. That's bothersome enough, but it also raises theological problems for our doctrine of the body. Is the human body inherently indecent?

Certainly not, but it can be inappropriately vulnerable, or misused, or debased, just as easily as it can be appropriately vulnerable, or limited in its vulnerability. When I was a teenager, our church youth group took two trips most summers: we took mission work trips to serve poor communities in Appalachia, and we went canoeing in the Boundary Waters of Minnesota. Coed groups of teenagers with our lovely bodies swam, sweated, and slept in close proximity to one another. We wore bathing suits and tank tops and the boys were often without shirts. We applied sunscreen and bug spray, and frequently smeared dirt across our arms, feet, and faces, and scratched ourselves silly when even the professional-grade DDT failed us and we inevitably got chomped by mosquitoes.

On those trips, sometimes kids paired off. There were

certainly individuals who would have inspired shudders of
anxious delight if they'd offered to rub in my SPF 30 . . .
but they were also the individuals who helped you when the
pack you'd picked up was too heavy, who handed you the
hammer to complete the gutter repair you were working on,
with whom you played cards deep into the night. The various physical intimacies were periodically fraught if there
was someone you "liked," but what made them appropriate
between nice, Christian-ish youth was that they were intimacies born of a common life and relationship. Sometimes
there was a charge, but more often our interactions were
simply part of life together.

As we get older, as our relationships turn from latent hor-
monal pining to actually romantic and sexual, this mundane
and holy comfort in our physical vulnerability can be a real
gift as we begin the difficult work of navigating the great un-
knowns: unknown power dynamics, unnamed assumptions,
unspoken desires. We are vulnerable, always—human—but
all the time I spent either naked or sweating around other
people helped me build resilience. That resilience, which different folks come by in different ways, buoys us in the tricky
work of knowing how to take risks, how to be vulnerable,
while being aware about how much potential for hurt we're
willing to take on.

WE ARE MISTAKEN, though, if we think vulnerability, especially
of the sexual variety, is only about bodies, about being literally naked. We're human: which means we have myriad
means of sharing ourselves. We have minds and souls and
words, too.

One night in grad school, a group of friends was hanging out in someone's room drinking wine and talking about music and poetry. Sitting on the floor in a corner by a bookshelf, I turned to peruse the shelves and pulled off a copy of the Billy Collins collection *Picnic, Lightning*. Billy Collins was big with me in grad school.

"I love him!" I said to our host, showing him the cover. I grabbed my bag, fished out my journal, and read the poem I'd copied down there recently, "Man in Space."

All you have to do is listen to the way a man
sometimes talks to his wife at a table of people
and notice how intent he is on making his point
even though her lower lip is beginning to quiver,

and you will know why the women in science
fiction movies who inhabit a planet of their own
are not pictured making a salad or reading a magazine
when the men from earth arrive in their rocket,

why they are always standing in a semicircle
with their arms folded, their bare legs set apart,
their breasts protected by hard metal disks.[13]

I finished, and there was a moment of silence. The women all knew that feeling; we had all experienced "mansplaining,"[14] we had all been hurt. We had, after all, each been in love, and each worked in churches. The poem reminded the young men sitting there of what sort of preexisting vulnerabilities a lot of women bring into relationships and vocations.

I love that poem, but I needed to lighten the mood. Hell,

we'd been talking about Shakira, she whose hips don't lie, before I started speaking of uncomfortable truths. So I cracked open *Picnic, Lightning* and read another of my favorite poems. "Victoria's Secret" describes a narrator's perusal of a recent lingerie catalog. He describes the various ensembles—the camisoles and teddies; the materials and the colors. He is both comic and ambivalently aroused, imagining what the models are supposed to be conveying with their expressions and postures.

> The one in the upper-left-hand corner
> is giving me a look
> that says I know you are here
> and I have nothing better to do
> for the remainder of human time
> than return your persistent but engaging stare.
> She is wearing a deeply scalloped
> flame-stitch halter top
> with padded push-up styling
> and easy side-zip tap pants.[15]

The poem goes on for stanza after stanza; I read it all aloud, sitting on the floor of my friend's room. I can tell you, more than a decade later, what I was wearing: my hair in two messy buns at the nape of my neck, my black, fitted, scoop-neck sweater. It's entirely possible that a modicum of cleavage was visible from the vantage point of others in the room, given my spot on the floor, and the fact that I almost always lean forward when I read aloud. At some point, I started to blush, but I also read with feeling and confidence.

The room grew warm. We laughed. We shifted in our seats.

That impromptu poetry reading surprised me; I felt like I was performing, but I also felt like I'd revealed something about myself. In reading and responding to Collins's words, I'd acknowledged myself as a sexual being. I felt vulnerable—*did I really just read a sexy poem aloud to a bunch of seminarians?*—but also really, really good. I felt seen, and it felt a little dangerous, but also kind of thrilling.

All that with words. Someone else's words, no less.

A few months later, still in my Billy Collins period, I started dating someone. A fellow student, he would write comments in the margins of my class notes as we listened to lectures on theological anthropology. We decided to go to a blues club, and I e-mailed him Collins's poem "The Blues." As poor grad students, we had a lot of study dates: we'd sit at his dining room table until we made enough progress on our course reading to go make out. He was older than me, and I was totally enamored. He thought I was "guarded," a bit of a "closed book," which I thought was absurd because I am totally incapable of keeping a secret about myself. Despite the fact that he had clearly misread me, and that he was a complete mystery to me, our physical relationship managed to advance, as these things sometimes do. (He was cute! We were grown-ups.) He did not think it was wise to sleep together. So we did not. But though that particular line was never crossed, I experienced the only shame I ever had in a romantic relationship. I felt too forward, misunderstood and unappreciated. I felt as though I had offered myself, and he had tried me on for size, and found me lacking.

Words are powerful, but the interplay of words and

bodies—of literally and figuratively baring ourselves—is perhaps most powerful, and potentially dangerous, of all.

I, along with much of the rest of America, recently read the young adult novel *The Fault in Our Stars*. I loved it, obviously. But the thing I loved most was when toward the end of the book (spoiler alert) the main characters, Hazel and Augustus, are about to go to bed together. She's suggested it, and they ride the elevator up to his hotel room, and then he stops in the hallway. She feels the anxiety rise in her chest; has she come on too strong? Does he think she's slutty or something? He takes a deep breath and describes the sight of his amputated leg. He is not ashamed of it, exactly, but it is his wound, his vulnerability made visible, and he wants to gauge her response while he can still bear it. If she recoils at the sight, it will be too much for him. She is relieved beyond measure. "Oh, *get over yourself.*"[16]

They have a connection, one built over conversation and mutual affection. They trust and love each other. And so while they take a risk (and, truly, only an emotional one, as the use of a condom is specifically mentioned), they are mutually vulnerable.

It's a lovely scene.

Just as in locating a Christian sexual ethic that works, articulating what "appropriate vulnerability" looks like depends hugely on context and the individuals involved. For some, who value highly reserving the most intimate sexual acts for marriage or the period immediately "pre-ceremony," any activities outside of that context might feel inappropriate; a risk not worth taking, regardless of how deeply in love the partners are. For others, who simply need a reasonable guarantee that they'll be treated well by a respectful and engaged partner, appropriate vulnerability might include quite a bit more activity.

Josh and I were together for less time than I had dated the Billy Collins boy when we started a sexual relationship. The leap felt less than perfectly responsible (though not by public health standards! We both live by the rule that hearts heal faster than HIV or herpes), but like a controlled fall nonetheless. I'd known him for over a year when we got together, and in every interaction with him, communication was simple: there were no crossed wires, we got each other's jokes, we appreciated each other's innuendos and advances. Our physical intimacy was a logical extension of the initial stages of our relationship, a continuing conversation carried out with hands and mouths and bodies instead of words.

Falling in love, opening myself, felt like stepping out in faith. It was faster than I previously would have thought could possibly be faithful, but I trusted him—and he trusted me. We had faith in *us*. We were both rendered vulnerable, and we received the gift of the other with thanksgiving.

I recently discovered a new poem by Mary Oliver that I just love—I read it to Josh, because it seemed to tell our story. It's funny, because it's kind of naughty. But I think it's a holy story, too.

> I did think, let's go about this slowly.
> This is important. This should take
> some really deep thought. We should take
> small, thoughtful steps.
>
> But, bless us, we didn't.[17]

We're all raised with different understandings of the multiple meanings of nakedness and human vulnerability. Our comfort levels and ability to balance protecting ourselves from undue harm and willingness to open ourselves also vary individually: my sisters, my mother, and I have different experiences, different ways of inhabiting our bodies and navigating our relationships. Learning to be naked and unashamed in our sexual relationships is possible, even though that freedom and courage will look different than in the relative innocence of childhood. It is my dear hope that marriages can be safe spaces to do this work—but the institution is no guarantee, any more than being unmarried is a guarantee of danger and pain. Married, partnered, or single, carrying with us a sexual ethic that takes our vulnerability into account can help us to breathe deeply of the charged air of sexual connection, while maintaining our integrity and self-care, so that we can all know the joy and assurance of self-revelation, union, and love.

Chapter Six

We Might Be Strangers

A Theology of Intimacy

Once upon a time, I had a friend. We spent a lot of time together one summer, left for different schools again in the fall, saw each other over the holidays. At some point in the heat of mini-golf excursions and trips for ice cream and conversation, I began to hope that we might be more than friends. And by that, I mean that I started listening even more obsessively than normal to Ani DiFranco (*So many sheep I quit counting / sleepless and embarrassed about the way that I feel*[1]), listening to my Walkman in bed on those hot summer nights, pining away and vehemently denying it when my parents asked if there was something going on between us.

Perhaps because the narrative in my family told of my parents' long-standing friendship that precipitated and undergirded their romance, perhaps because I'd memorized *When Harry Met Sally*, I never had a hard time believing that friends could get together; in fact, I was pretty convinced friendship was a critical part of romance. If you didn't *like* the other person, how could you *like like* them?

But "I only like you as a friend" was a common enough rejection in our circles. Long before men complained on the Internet about the treachery of the "friend zone," I inhabited it. Couldn't he see that we had something more? Couldn't he see that I wanted him to take my hand? He wrote me letters that fall—was this a sign? Or just a throwback habit for aspiring writers?

We went to a party one night over winter break. Not one night—New Year's Eve. We drank, but did not drive. As we were walking to a cab, emboldened by intoxication, I stopped him. *Listen. If we weren't friends, would you be attracted to me?* Sure, he said.

Well. Do you think that even though we're friends, you could kiss me? Because it's New Year's, and I haven't been kissed yet.

He backed me up against a wall and kissed me. It was hot. Definitely maybe something he'd been thinking about doing for a while.

We said good night. He went back to school before we saw each other again.

A few months later I took the Greyhound to his school for the weekend. Just a friend visiting a friend. No subtext or anything. We ice-skated. We must have eaten, though I have absolutely no memory of that. We went to a party. We played beer pong, as you do. We went back to his apartment, sat on the couch in thick silence. And went to bed. I slept on a borrowed mattress, by myself.

He hugged me when I got on the bus to go back to Boston, but that was that.

At some point later, I asked him why nothing happened that weekend, why he'd never kissed me again, especially not over those days with so much opportunity. "We'd been drinking. I didn't think anything should happen if we weren't sober."

As it happened, we were not in the same city again for almost a year, by which time we'd both started to date others. The moment passed and the window closed. Since emerging from the haze of my pining, I have never regretted that this boy and I didn't end up dating. We would have been a terrible couple. And, in fact, I have been grateful that he was wise enough to see what I couldn't: that alcohol can helpfully lower our inhibitions, can, when the moment arises, press the shy and nervous into action, but can also ultimately prove a crutch to the sort of intimacy that friendship and love require.

My months of pining for this boy were neither my first nor my only experience with unrequited affection. I specialized in those conversational moments when the transition from friendly flirtation could have moved to physical connection, and didn't. In those myriad moments, I wished, wished, the fellow in question could simply read my mind. *I want you to kiss me.*

The desire to be seen and known, to be intimately understood, is central to the human experience, and certainly to the Christian longing for God, but so is its flip side. The idea of grace, or unmerited love and forgiveness, is so attractive and marvelous because many of us feel that, if anyone really knew us, or saw us at our ugliest, those all-seeing eyes would know once and for all that we were disgusting and petty and narcissistic and afraid. To be seen as we really are, we might fear, would render us unworthy of love, would make it impossible for anyone to want to make out with us, much less build a life with us. We desire intimacy in a number of ways—emotionally in our friendships, our families, spiritually in whatever way we worship the divine, and physically with a lover. In this chapter, we'll look at what intimacy is not—not a mind-meld, not a once-and-for-always connection—and what it is: an opening ourselves up to be changed through relationship, in, we hope, holy and life-giving ways.

WHENEVER I THINK about spiritual intimacy, or intimacy with the divine, Psalm 139 comes to mind, something I have read for comfort and poetry, but which also freaks me out a bit: "O Lord, you have searched me and known me . . . Where can I go from your spirit? Or where can I flee from your presence?" (Psalm 139:1, 7). Does that include the bathroom? I sometimes wonder. Or the corner of my mind where I shove my ungenerous, self-righteous thoughts? Or my bedroom, especially when I'm having sex?

If I get too far along that train of thought, I remind myself that intimacy with the divine is different, as the Lord God is no Peeping Tom. The Living God is, rather, that force that moves in and through me; the spirit in me that is best, and most loving, the mystery of grace. When I feel a judging eye, it emerges less from a wrathful dude somewhere, and more from the sense of an estrangement from who I am created to be; it's feeling apart from the source of my life and the ground of my identity because of some sin I'm committing or some gross thing I'd rather not admit to.

There's a history in Christian thought of describing sex—holy, good sex—as sacramental; a point of ecstatic connection with our partner, a collapsing of the distance that separates us from all other people, and even a collapsing of the distance between humanity and God. We often talk about different forms of love: "agape" is the grace-filled neighbor love we aspire to; "philia" is "brotherly" or familiar love. "Eros" is about communion. Union. The desire to join with another. We know this word. We witness eros depicted in art, poetry, film, music. It's the popular love; we hear a lot less about agape on Top 40 radio.

Christian mystics have experienced God in ways that can only be described as erotic throughout the centuries: moments of vision or ecstasy in which they feel drawn in by the Divine Love. Mechthild of Magdeburg (c. 1210–1297 CE) wrote,

Lord, now I am a naked soul
And you in yourself an All-Glorious God.
Our mutual intercourse
Is eternal life without end.[2]

This language is strange and somewhat disconcerting if we think of God as the bearded fellow who creepily watches us all the time. But, as Bernard McGinn, scholar of medieval mysticism, once argued, "the mystics contend that divine love is the heart of all reality."[3]

"The use of certain forms of erotic expression [is] for a different purpose—the transformation of all human desires in terms of what the mystic believes to be its true source."[4] That is, the divine reality, "God," is the source and end ("telos," or purpose) of love; that love reaches out to and moves through and is experienced by humanity, and can even transform human love, rendering it in service to the divine love that gave it its power in the first place. In those ecstatic experiences, the soul is known, naked, and brought into union with its source. The language is erotic; the experience is intimate.

Though I believe in the possibility of ecstatic communion between God and humanity, and certainly of the communion of bodies and souls possible in intimate acts and relationships between humans, I think those experiences can be hard to come by.

Intimacy with the divine has been cultivated throughout history through prayer, ritual, meditation, discernment. The transformation of our loves into service of the divine love is a lifelong endeavor. Whether we experience that intimacy as comfort and peace, ecstasy and passion, or something in between, will depend on who we are and the type of our deepest longings. Do we need peace? Do we long for passion?

INTIMACY WITH OTHER human beings seems different, first and foremost because those of us who long for intimacy with the divine tend to profess that we know things about the character of God. God is infinitely trustworthy; God graciously receives our longings; God forgives all our shortcomings. God will not fail to return our calls if we come off as too needy. We relate to God as the fabric of reality, the source of our Life, the One who moves within and through us. Other people require that you put your thoughts into words most of the time; other people are not merely mysterious to us, they are strange.

Connecting fully with another person is often no easy task. And, worse, the ease of a physical connection does not always translate into an emotional one; a spiritual connection does not always lend itself to a romantic one.

One night, just after I'd started dating the Billy Collins guy, he walked with me across a city parking lot that separated the movie theater and the nearby wine bar where we were heading for a post-cinematic drink. (Not being able to afford dinner *and* a movie on a grad school student budget, we were still trying to keep it classy.) Snow started to fall, and he stopped in his tracks, took my hand, pulled me to him, and kissed me for the first time in the glow of the lamplight.

It was straight out of a romantic comedy; I half expected the soundtrack to swell.

In his arms, in the snow: that was the movie moment I'd been waiting for. The flirting and speculation and hyperarticulate conversation of two students in theology (for God's sake) finally led to action.

I swooned. *Atta boy!*

The elements of that kiss—the romance and the snow, plus the fact that this boy was a mainline Protestant graduate student just like me, had me well-nigh convinced that this one was the one that was going to stick. Whether I had the fates or providence to thank mattered little to me; I was just glad to be there.

But, to my great disappointment, that one moment was easily the most successful moment of our brief relationship (academic quarters are only ten weeks at the University of Chicago, so while we started in the snow, we were definitely done by spring break). A moment, even a singularly hot one, does not a life-lasting love make. We were always much better at reading each other's bodies than minds.

For all the hope and possibility of having a universe simply pulsing with Love, it's harder work than we, at the cusp of adulthood and sexual awakening, tend to realize. I don't just want to blame the romantic comedies for our bewilderment: there's also the Spice Girls (remember "2 Become 1"?) and the Bible.

Then the man said,
"This at last is bone of my bones
    and flesh of my flesh;
this one shall be called Woman,
    for out of Man this one was taken."
Therefore a man leaves his father and his mother and
    clings to his wife, and they become one flesh.

(GENESIS 2:23–24)

Paul uses that last verse to remind the folks at the church in Corinth not to sleep with prostitutes: "Do you not know that whoever is united to a prostitute becomes one body with her? For it is said, 'The two shall be one flesh'"

(1 Corinthians 6:16). He's like a first-century version of that terrible youth group abstinence activity: the one with the cup that everybody spits in; or the one with the tape that gets less sticky over time.

I've always wrestled with the "one flesh" phrasing. It's descriptive about certain acts, to be sure, and captures the erotic desire of lovers to be as closely intertwined as they possibly can be. But there is a distinct difference between actually losing the boundaries of one's self and the ecstatic joining of hearts and bodies that sometimes happens in the best sex. What we want to aim for, what we sometimes get, is deep, intimate connection, not the annihilation of parts of ourselves. The language in Genesis and used by Paul is metaphorical. Just as in mysticism, the drive "is toward a moment in which the difference between lover and beloved is extinguished."[5] When it happens, it's a wonder, but it lasts only a moment.

"You and I," a love song by the band Wilco, illustrates this phenomenon beautifully: *You and I, we might be strangers / however close we get sometimes.* We can swap bodily fluids, we can spend hours wrapped in the arms of another, we can learn her lines and curves as well as we know our own, but we can never read his mind.

My parents have been married, pretty happily, for close to forty years. They know each other better than anyone; sometimes, it seems, better than they know themselves. But there are times when one of them is in a funk, when one is overly anxious, when I ask, "Hey, what's up with [your beloved spouse]?" Close to forty years, and the response is still, often enough, *I have no idea.*

The same is true of Josh and me. We can periodically finish each other's sentences, but just as often I ask him what he's thinking. That's less frustrating than you'd think: it is good to still be able to be surprised. It is hot—soul-stirring—to ask and receive, to learn what the other wants, in her own words, from his own lips.

In the film *What Women Want* (2000), chauvinistic advertising executive Nick Marshall (Mel Gibson) acquires the ability to hear the thoughts of any women in the vicinity. For the viewer, it's an interesting look at the nature of intimacy. This proves to be a curse, then a blessing, then an opportunity for personal growth. But before that, Nick sees it as an opportunity to get laid.

There are huge problems with the film's premise; there are some jokes that ought not be made. You can tell the difference sixteen years have made in terms of what's acceptable. But there's an interesting insight on intimacy as our misguided protagonist romances the local barista. On a date, Nick's told Lola (Marisa Tomei) everything she wants to hear. She invites him up, but once they're half-naked and kissing, he finds himself distracted by her critical inner monologue. He tries to ram his tongue down her throat; he apparently does not appreciate that her breasts are attached and ought not be grabbed *and* twisted. She wonders which celebrity will be appearing on the late-night show, and if they'll be done in time for her to catch the broadcast.

Nick needs to regroup, and does, successfully. He starts to listen to Lola, and his responsiveness leads to heart-pounding, sweat-inducing, ecstatically marvelous sex. She reels: "Amazing! Ohhh! It was like, you were more inside me than anybody. Ever! I mean more inside my head! Like, you knew what I wanted and how I wanted it . . . We connected in a way that was beyond . . . beyond!"

Ecstatically mind-blowing sex is certainly something to aspire to, but even though Nick has a deeply personal (problematic, somewhat violating) perspective on Lola's needs and desires, theirs wouldn't exactly qualify as an intimate relationship. Or, if you buy the notion that conversation, that give and take, is erotic, neither is theirs particularly hot.

Intimacy requires mutuality: mutual vulnerability, mutual disclosure and openness, mutual invitation and consent (obvious, but worth stating). Mutuality in turn requires two distinct selves, which can be in relationship with each other. If, as Oscar Wilde suggests, "the essence of romance is uncertainty,"[6] romantic intimacy depends on the risk-taking step of opening ourselves to someone else. Psychologist and marriage counselor Harriet Lerner states:

> Intimacy means that we can be who we are in a relationship, and allow the other person to do the same. "Being who we are" requires that we can talk openly about the things that are important to us, that we take a clear position on where we stand on important emotional issues, and that we clarify the limits of what is acceptable and tolerable to us in a relationship. "Allowing the other person to do the same" means that we can stay emotionally connected to that other party who thinks, feels, and believes differently, without needing to change, convince, or fix the other.[7]

That part about "allowing the other person to do the same" often proves particularly challenging, especially as we seek to be in a relationship with someone who is not just individually different from us, in that way all selves are, but who's a different gender, or practices a different religion, or grew up in a different cultural milieu. Most people like to believe that their own view of reality is the best one . . . if they're even aware that theirs is only one of many. Lerner notes this seemingly obvious, but often overlooked fact: "People *are* different. *All of us see the world through a different filter, creating as many views of reality as there are people in it.*"[8]

We usually get that intellectually, but emotionally? That's another story entirely. This reality feels threatening; if someone's filter is different from ours and carries some truth; does that mean our filter is somehow less valid? In our early adulthood, figuring out what our personal filter is in the first place is hard, and tends to create no small amount of ambivalence before we even attempt to consider how it relates to the worldviews and habits of others.

It's not just romantic relationships that cause us trouble. In the midst of the decrescendo of a recent disagreement with my father-in-law, I had an epiphany. "John! You think, as the parent, you are meant to support us forever. That ours is a one-directional relationship. But in *my* family, we tend to think we're mutually obligated to care for each other over generations." Once we figured out our differing assumptions, we were able to make sense of what we were arguing about in the first place.

COMPLICATING THE MATTER of intimacy and acceptance is that each and every person is different, and puts their filter together in different ways.

One of the most irritating things about the church is when it traffics in stereotypes about men and women. Women are faithful and emotional and nurturing; men are leaders, but can't control their sex drives. This is irritating because these claims derive from lousy theology and cultural convention, but also because they claim to be strictly biblical when they're not. I know plenty of men for whom monogamy comes easily and women who are challenged by it. Nurturing men and assertive women. Women who love physical affection and intimacy as a means of expressing love, and men who could talk about their feelings *all night long, baby*. Men and women, straight and gay, and everybody in between, we all speak different love languages; our attempts at intimacy are hindered when we cling too closely to narrow scripts for who we are supposed to be. We stumble not because of our inherent differences, but because, as Lerner notes, of "our reactivity to differences," and the ways in which our "reactivity exaggerates and calcifies differences."[9]

Scripts can be oppressive; the unknown can be paralyzing.

No wonder we experience intimacy as both terrifying and exhilarating. To face uncertainty, the risk of rejection, the vulnerability of connection, head-on and act: that takes courage. Many of us are aware of that but, not knowing from what source we might draw it, settle on the illusion of courage, or do our best to otherwise distance ourselves from the risk involved. Some folks chemically, if temporarily, banish their inhibitions. Some retreat into relationships that can't possibly be intimate, with sex workers or strangers, or varied pornographic media.

If we remember the ethical language from chapter three, these failures of courage provide a critique of an overreliance on fantasy or pornography, or of "hookup culture." If sex is for the appropriate practice and experience of vulnerability, then repeated behaviors that mask that purpose are unethical. I've always wondered what to do with the apostle Paul's condemnation of "fornication" in that letter to the church at Corinth (6:18 in particular). In the Greek, it's *porneia*." In the new Common English Bible, it's "sexual immorality." Fornication is traditionally seen as extramarital sex. But that seems both overly broad and overly narrow. *Porneia* includes just about every naughty thing you can think of, including sex with relatives and animals, but also some that seem categorically "not like the others" to our modern ears (i.e., sex with someone who has been divorced). "Sexual immorality" is similarly all-inclusive, and unhelpfully vague. What makes something immoral?

If, like some of my survey respondents, I used erotica[10] with my partner, or we got a little drunk on our anniversary, would that be a problem? I think, as with most things in Christian ethics, the question is not about the nature of the act itself, but the intent and the effect of the action. The use of erotica or a little alcohol might help a committed couple to explore their sexual relationship together, to ease some tension, help him last longer, increase the likelihood of laughing together. The question then is, does the action serve the purpose of deepening intimacy and self-knowledge?

Masturbation (or, as we've determined to be the nicer-sounding terms, solo sex or self-stimulation) is another great example of how critical context can be in considering the ethical status of an act; in the first chapter, we explored it as a means to discussing pleasure. It's worth revisiting now for what it can reveal about the nature of intimacy. The sex columnist Dan Savage routinely gets letters from guys who are accustomed to a certain amount of self-love, administered with a particular grip.[11] Sometimes these letter writers find themselves losing their erections in the warmer, moister, softer climes of their partner, and they fret about that. Savage inevitably tells them to back off a bit, loosen their grip, try some other things. Reengaging their partners, opening themselves to different sexual approaches and environs, will help them to keep their erections and will open the door to greater intimacy with their partners. It is no trick, one could say, to help oneself achieve orgasm. The right hand not only knows what the left hand is doing, but is usually working in concert with all one's other parts. There are no barriers in communication, no space between selves to navigate. If you want intimacy in addition to an orgasm, you have to slow down and learn to communicate.

That's not to say that masturbation is always a problem for men, and that solo sex isn't a great, free, safe way to experience pleasure. As Christine Gudorf writes: "There is seldom any recognition [in much current Christian conversation] that intimacy with one's own body is possible; there is even less recognition that a good is at stake."[12]

Sometimes it can become a roadblock to intimacy and

mutual pleasure in the way Savage describes, especially for men. But paradoxically, masturbation can be an important aid for women in defining themselves, their needs and their desires, which is critical for the building of intimacy. Two complete selves are required, we recall, for intimacy. If she doesn't know who she is, or what she likes, or what she wants, how can she share that with her partner?

Gudorf reports:

> While many fewer women masturbate as adolescents, those who do are more likely to be sexually successful within partnered sex because of greater self-knowledge. The turn to solitary sex in adolescence actually seems to facilitate and not to impede learning to turn to others for the meeting of physical and sexual desires and needs.[13]

Context matters, and in figuring out how it ought to matter to the ordering of our romantic and sexual lives, it's important to consider how that context relates to what we consider faithful norms. What constitutes sexual immorality?

In *What Women Want*, Lola and Nick have sex on their first date. Such a thing has been known to happen in real life, and I'm not convinced (even as a pastor) that the act is, in itself, necessarily immoral. What makes it ethically problematic at the beginning is that he sees sex as an opportunity to perform, to stroke his own ego, and to derive personal pleasure without any particular regard for her pleasure; it lacks mutuality. But the onus does not rest solely on him; Lola was passionately engaged in their foreplay, but when things become less pleasurable, she critiques her partner snarkily and then checks out.

It's a way of protecting herself, I bet. (And now I will stop psychologizing a movie character.) Gudorf reminds us that the power of sex lies largely in the pleasure it brings. There's pleasure in desire, in arousal, in exploring and kissing, of course. But sex aims to end in orgasm, a pleasure so intense and laden with potential meaning that descriptions tend toward the metaphorical. To speak of an orgasm as a contraction of muscles and a crescendo of heart rate and blood flow doesn't really capture the sense of standing outside oneself, outside of time. Sometimes referred to as "a little death," an orgasm is an experience of letting go of control and self-consciousness. Yet it manifests a strange paradox, too: one usually can't will an orgasm absent any physical stimulation, but the physical isn't usually sufficient, either—for men or women. To be carried away "often demands a kind of conscious, deliberate, letting go of control over oneself and one's reactions, a willingness to immerse oneself in the sensation."[14]

The pleasure we take from sex, then, is tied in a number of ways to our ability to feel safe when at our most vulnerable and to our willingness to let go of control and self-consciousness. That's not exactly the same as obliterating that which separates us from our partner—sex need not be an ecstatic and divine experience of unity with all creation in order to be considered *good*. Indeed, the frequency with which a pair reaches orgasm simultaneously suggests that such a thing cannot be the primary end of sex. (For that matter, if we're talking about divine intention and design, the design of the clitoris suggests that women were designed for pleasure, but not necessarily for deriving said pleasure from heterosexual intercourse.)

This insight, though, helps to make sense of the research done by Donna Freitas, a Roman Catholic theologian who studies hookup culture on American college campuses.[15] A self-described feminist, Freitas began her work a few years ago when she questioned several thousand college students at several types of colleges and universities about their sex lives. Many reported that a culture of "random" or nonmonogamous sexual activity reigned at their schools (save the evangelical colleges). Freitas's work is limited dramatically by the wide scope of activities she includes in her definition of "hooking up": anything from kissing to intercourse. While kissing strangers isn't for everyone, the level of intimacy, trust, and vulnerability inherent in a kiss on a dance floor is hugely different from nailing half the campus, or even just that girl from your psych class, if only from a public health standpoint.

But the great insight of her work is that a number of students who reported participating in hookup culture also reported their ambivalence about it, and many who were having actual sex (oral, penis-in-vagina, or anal) weren't particularly satisfied with the *quality* of the sex they were having. Freitas is funny: she feels sad for these "sexually liberated" students who are having terrible sex. If you're going to be "liberated," she marvels, shouldn't you at least be enjoying it?

Hers is a good and important question. It's easy to see

why the sex isn't always very good: for those who feel ambivalent about the culture in which they find themselves,
and yet haven't honed in on a way to opt out, it makes sense
that they should drink to numb their doubts, or disengage
to decrease their emotional and physical vulnerability. And
sex, without the dance of intimacy, is just not very much
fun; "bumping uglies" is about as far from transcendence as
you can get.

Freitas wants to reclaim abstinence—total abstinence,
or temporary seasons of abstinence—from the extremes
of religious finger-wagging. Students should go on dates.
She commends small groups of students who take pride
in their virginity, and refuse to be shamed for their sexual
inexperience.[16]

There's surely some good advice there—dates *can be*
awesome—but it seems strange to me that the prescription
for a failure to navigate intimacy and vulnerability would
be to abstain from the learning curve. She's trying to lower
the stakes, maybe—test out intimacy through conversation
first—but why "abstinence"? Why not *only sleep with people
you think are interesting* or *experiment with speaking up with
your partner about what you like?*

As CHRISTIANS, OUR preoccupation with abstinence arises,
I think, from a desire to talk about how sex is important:
meaningful, special, and sacred. And sex is often those
things. But it seems one of the only arguments we've got
against promiscuity, or any extramarital exercise of our
sexuality, is related to Paul's 1 Corinthians admonishment,
something I call the "Horcrux defense." In the Harry Potter

universe, a Horcrux is a magical object that can be created only through the darkest magic. It's a means of grasping at immortality, of stowing a portion of one's soul in an object. To make one requires a murder, and both that act and the subsequent dividing of one's soul compromise the integrity of the individual's soul. A soul ought not be divided.

Now, we mostly don't equate sex with murder,[17] but more often than not Christians talk about sex as giving a part of ourselves away, as creating an irrevocable bond with any and all partners we've had, as inviting ourselves to be changed, or defiled, by the characteristics of those partners. It's not something we want to share with just anyone. It's not something we want to have too much of outside of a monogamous marital relationship.

Sex is, of course, an important and meaningful thing—with the potential to heal hearts and blow up bridges, as we've noted—but I want to stop and consider for a moment what theological questions arise from the Horcrux defense. First: Can our "selves" be divided, defiled, or otherwise diminished? If so, what can accomplish such a thing? So, too, we should ask: Are we forever bonded with whomever we've shared a physically intimate interaction with? And, relatedly: Isn't it totally jerky to be like, *I'm too good for sex with that person*?

Sex—intimacy—opens us up to change. It asks us to trust and let go, to relax and experiment. It draws us into play and pleasure, but also the work of communicating with another person who cannot get inside our heads. Through sex we can practice attention, invitation, hospitality, and the means of grace. As Gudorf says, "When sex is not segregated from the rest of our lives, the pleasure of orgasm can reach far beyond the moment of intense pleasure itself, and change, a little at a time, the way we relate to our partner, and even to the larger society and the world. It can encourage us to trust more, to be willing to risk more, to reach out to others in love."[18]

When sex is segregated from the rest of our lives—when it is understood as something that must be set apart to be kept holy, when our sexuality is treated as something we can divorce from the rest of our selves, kept in a box until we're ready to use it within marriage—we misunderstand the critical importance of context in shaping ethics and a holy, healthy life.

Our holiness, our worth, our identity as image-bearers of God, is not compromised through the attempt to grow in love and intimacy with those around us. Our worth is not something we can give away; it's something we're supposed to share with others. Voldemort, the one who divides and divides himself, is barely human anymore; *our* humanity can never be diminished, no matter how many sexual partners we've had. We're created to be in relationship, after all. It's not sex outside of marriage that threatens us; it's our fear of living and growing in intimacy with others. It's our unwillingness to open ourselves up to the abundance of life's created goodness—to wonder and mystery and pleasure and relationship—that often leaves us feeling empty.

The call of the gospel is not to protect ourselves at all costs, but to risk ourselves in love. Not always, not with the whole rugby team or all the ladies in the marketing department, but nonetheless with hope, wisdom, and courage.

The call of the gospel, too, is to actively refrain from dismissing anyone as outside of the circle of God's care. Jesus healed bleeding women who were ritually impure; Jesus responded with gratitude to the extravagant and intimate gesture from the woman who washed his feet with costly oil and her hair (whether she was "a sinner" or his friend "Mary of Bethany" is lost to history; Luke says one, John says another; Jesus accepts the loving gift either way). These and other stories in the Gospels serve as important reminders to a culture rife with double standards about sexual experience as an admirable and enviable quality in men and a source of shame and sign of moral laxity in women.

True intimacy requires us to eschew those double standards and to transcend our assumptions about others. We cannot read minds; we have to learn to be in conversation with our partners—not just about shared sexual experience, but about our feelings, our hopes, fears, and interests. Coming to know another person intimately, in body, mind, and soul, is exhilarating and joy-filled, even as it can be terrifying to open ourselves up, to be seen and known in new ways. We may have a host of intimate relationships of varied types throughout our lives; if we are lucky, sharing and seeing will be a blessed adventure. It is not always so, however.

The last theological assumption of the Horcrux defense instructs that we ought to limit our number of partners because sex inevitably binds us to another in lasting ways. We should try to avoid the breaking of our hearts because they are subsequently less capable of opening widely and deeply to our future spouse; we should avoid placing claims on people who will one day belong to someone else. The exploration of that claim opens the next chapter. How do we talk about the meaning of love and sex, and the possibility of intimacy and right relationship, when many of us have been in love more than once? How do we navigate the kind of world in which my mother found herself saying, "You may not invite anyone you have slept with to your wedding"? How do we claim and make sense of the past in ways that allow us to live with courage in the present and with hope for the future?

Chapter Seven

History

A Theology of Exes and the Things That Once Were

Memory is a funny beast.

When "Blurred Lines" came out in 2013, I listened to it almost every time it came on the radio, as long as my kids weren't in the car. As a feminist, as someone concerned about the pervasiveness of rape culture, as someone who found the nods to that rape culture particularly egregious in rapper T.I.'s contribution to the bridge (*I'm a nice guy, but . . .* is both the most and least offensive line), I cannot defend this. But I loved the hook, I loved the homage to Motown soul, and I loved Thicke's rhetorical question *What do they make dreams for / When you got them jeans on?*

It reminded me of the first time I spent a long night

dancing with someone I was hot for in a club with cheap drinks and great music. It reminded me of feeling his hand on my waist and wondering if we were just dancing or if he felt what I felt. It reminded me of those blurred lines of friendship and attraction and dancing and desire.

It reminded me of the joke that Christians don't approve of sex because it might lead to dancing. Which of course is funny because Christians often fear that dancing might lead to sex; which is funny because often at least one dance partner wants it to, if not immediately than eventually. Dancing can be foreplay.

That's what "Blurred Lines" felt like to me—why I loved it and kept it from my children: crass, but fun, foreplay.

Memory is a terrible beast.

Those who have heard "I know you want it" and "I'm a nice guy, but . . ." and "I'm going to *do* this *to* you" spoken to them before acts of violence and coercion might understandably have quite a different response to the song.

I have never had acts of violence or coercion visited upon me, but certain words can stop me in my tracks and cart me off somewhere I'd rather not go: words that will never make it into my personal vocabulary of dirty talk and naughty slang; compliments that I'd rather not receive. I remember the first time I felt sick to my stomach when an older man made a comment about my legs. I remember, too, sitting in Mrs. Smith's eighth-grade reading classroom after school, making up a missed reading period, while another student served a detention. Alone in the room with me, he filled the forty-five minutes with vulgar questions and suggestions. I sat in silent shock, hoping that if I didn't acknowledge him he'd stop. (What girl isn't told to ignore them to get them to leave you alone?) I'd never had anyone talk to me that way before; never heard anyone talk that way, never had another living soul reference my genitalia. He took the same route home on the late bus afterward, and I remember sitting near the front, intentionally close to the creepy driver, who was a safer bet for neutral conversation. The boy, whose name I never recall, but whose leering face I could still pick out in my junior high yearbook, didn't say another word to me.

That afternoon I got home, desperately hoping my parents would read my mind, so they would know something had happened without me having to find words or give voice to how disgusting I felt. At thirteen, I had already started to imagine what it would be like to kiss or be with a boy; I wanted someone to see and know me. I had not wanted this, though I worried that I had invited it by wanting the other attention.

It's not much of a violation as far as violations go. I climbed into bed earlier, pulled the covers over my head, cried, and went to sleep.

What do we do with our sexual and romantic histories? What do we make of the parts we hate, of the sins and crimes committed against us that seem unlimited in their capacity to injure again and again? How do we hold the memories that continue to inspire our ambivalence, or our regret over hurts we've caused? And what do we do with the things that were wonderful, but are gone? Are we forever bound to the experiences and individuals who have populated our past?

Time is a central concern in Christian thought: how we

live in it, how we understand it, how God moves in it and beyond it. That's what I want to explore in this chapter: how time, memory, forgiveness, and hope go together as we seek to reconcile what we've seen and done, who we've been, with who we long to be. For most of us, our current relationship is not our first rodeo. What do we make of what has come before, what was delightful and what was dreadful?

God's grace can be a critical source of healing in all of that, but we mustn't allow platitudes or calls for quick forgiveness—for reconciliation where there is none—to masquerade as that grace. We're called to reflective engagement with our own stories, as well as the unfolding of God's story through history. Our hope is that we'll know salvation—not in some distant heaven, but even here, even now.

MANY PEOPLE THINK of time, of history, as, in the words of Winston Churchill, "one damn thing after another." It is simply the unfolding of things, the way we measure how it is that everything doesn't happen all at once. But humanity has ascribed different meanings to this unfolding: imagined that the gods or the fates have arranged all things from time immemorial or, alternatively, suggested that time itself is fully relative, passing differently in space, passing differently for children than adults.

Our views of the past, present, and future reveal and shape not simply what we think about the world, but how we come to terms with our own personal histories. Everybody loves a good redemption narrative: Christian worship, particularly American evangelical worship, has long featured the sharing of testimony—of lives once a disaster, until the surrender to Christ's lordship. But this is no new story: John Newton wrote *I once was lost, but now am found / Was blind, but now I see* in 1779; the apostle Paul saw the risen Christ, was blinded, and had the scales fall from his eyes just a few years before that. The Hebrew Bible narratives are divided into the exilic and post-exilic periods: from the period following the destruction of the Temple and the time spent living in a strange new land, in a foreign culture, to the time when they returned to their homeland and tried to rebuild.

Christians have even structured our calendar this way, marking years not from our perceived beginning of recorded time, but as periods of "before and after"; before and after the advent of our Lord. Time, we understand, includes all the happenings, large and small, under the sun, but is also marked by significant moments of change, of possibility, of pain.

The Psalmist prays:

Be mindful of your mercy, O Lord, and of your
    steadfast love,
    for they have been from of old.
Do not remember the sins of my youth or my
    transgressions;
    according to your steadfast love remember me,
    for your goodness' sake, O Lord!

(PSALM 25:6–7)

Remember this, but don't remember that. God requests similar responses from the people: remember that you were exiles; remember my promises; do not remember your old ways. Jesus, too: "You have heard it said . . . , but I say to you."

The relationship of the divine to humanity is character-ized by this back-and-forth, by remembering and forgetting, by forgiving and retelling, by change and reinterpretation. History is, in some ways, one damn thing after another, but also, now in Mark Twain's witty phrasing, "History never repeats itself, but it often rhymes." I even hear the voice of God, weary of the Israelites' continued breaking of the cov-enant, or Jesus, as the people routinely miss his point, in Edna St. Vincent Millay: "It's not true that life is one damn thing after another; it's one damn thing over and over."

MY MEMORY OF dancing is still called to mind by Top 40 radio, but I only recall the longing and desire I felt; I remember *that* I felt longing and desire all those years ago. But the feelings don't themselves remain. That distance took some time. Bob Dylan names it well in his song "Most of the Time" eventually singing: *Don't even remember what her lips felt like on mine.*[1]

It wasn't always that way. When I was lonely in grad school following a breakup, flailing in classes, I could call the happy memory of dancing with a London friend and crush to mind, with all its erotic pathos, and start pining with renewed vigor. My memory served to distract me from my current mess. What if, I could muse, I had actually made a move? We danced around getting together for years, and it was only when Josh and I started dating, and the London boy married his longtime love, that we stopped keeping in touch. The memory stayed, but the feelings faded, because the uncertainty, that what-ifs, the revisionist fantasies were gone. There was no uncertainty; we were certainly with other people. The door had certainly closed.

I once read a book written by an earnest young Christian man, who had married a woman who had multiple sexual partners "before becoming a Christian." He lamented the way he felt the ghosts of those previous lovers haunting their marital bed—was she comparing them? Was she longing for the past? I couldn't believe the way he seemed to be blaming her for his own insecurity.

Surely there are those who will compare one partner with another—or will use past relationships as measuring sticks by which to evaluate current ones (or, worse, will evaluate real partners based on fictional characters or porn). But I think that's poor behavior and bad habits more than the necessary consequence of having had more than one relationship.

I officiated a wedding once for a gorgeous and wonderful couple who were active members of a thriving, progressive church, two thoughtful people in their late twenties who couldn't have been more in love. In one of our counseling sessions, though, the bride mentioned that she had some lingering anxiety about the fact that he had lived with a previous girlfriend. Neither bride nor groom were "saving themselves for marriage," but there was something about the cohabitation that bothered her. It was too close to marriage: the domesticity, the quotidian nature of the sex with his previous partner. She was jealous.

Topping things off, he was still Facebook friends with his ex, and pictures yet existed of them as a couple. He tried to reassure her: their relationship was so much more; he loved her so deeply. But that first woman had been an important part of his life, once. He felt strange not acknowledging that. Still, his memory of her was distant. *Don't even remember what her lips felt like on mine.*

His bride relaxed, in the assurance of his love, and in the grace that fades memories and replaces them. Sex and domesticity for him now, and for as long as he could remember and foresee, was about the two of them.

There are those who worry about the long-term effects of the pervasive sexual assault, the imperfect intimacies of hookups, the marriages of those who have sexual and romantic histories (and the inevitable threat to them posed by the Facebook bogeyman). Me? While I'm fascinated by longitudinal studies, I don't worry too much about the long-term effects of a lengthy sexual and romantic learning curve. I do worry about a culture of pervasive sexual violence, of course, but I also have hope in the ability of survivors to overcome even the deepest darkness. At the same time, I've known too many folks in recovery and too many friends who can't quite shake bad relationships to believe that once we've seen the light, we'll never struggle again. I'm moved by the poetry of *I once was lost, but now am found / Was blind, but now I see,* but am convinced it's truer as a metaphor than as a diagnostic tool.

I don't believe in inevitable progress, but I do believe in the steadfast grace of God, the love that will not let us go, the hope that God's time is ever transforming me and you and the world toward love. I know women and men who were made to suffer but who know life again, and know it in abundance of joy.

I used to work in the same neighborhood in which I attended grad school, and even now, I am back regularly enough: teaching classes, attending conferences, spending too much money at the great bookstores. From the stop sign at 55th and Dorchester, I can see the apartment of the boy who mystified and confounded me, and the parking spot he sent me walking back to unexpectedly—alone! late!—after one of our dates.

At one of the chapels on campus, right before worship, two weeks after we broke up, he returned an errant sock of mine he'd finally managed to locate in his bedroom. It had, you can imagine, been misplaced in the heat of a moment deeply unlike the one that precedes community worship. The irony was jarring. The jerk. He even smiled as he handed it to me.

After we broke up, this lovely chapel became associated with my humiliation and my hurt. It's been more than a decade now; the building has undergone a renovation since then. But it's neither the design changes, nor the mere passage of time, nor even the frequency of my visits to the space that have provided healing, that have allowed me to set aside the association. It's what I've done in the space since then: I've worshipped, shared communion and Communion, preached and presided over memorials and weddings there. I've imposed ashes—confessed my sins and experienced assurance—at the beginning of Lent each year.

SAD, WISTFUL, WHAT-MIGHT-HAVE-BEEN memories are one thing. The pangs of heartbreak, no matter how severe, are of a different order from the weights burdening far too many people—if not you, then surely someone you know. What do we do with experiences in which things we value highly—trust, innocence, bodily integrity, hope, physical expressions of love and intimacy—are violated? What do we do when words of grace—*you are special, you are beautiful*—are twisted and turned, used in service of evil?

What of the girls and boys who are molested and raped at church, by pillars of the community? What damage is wrought in those whose first experiences of romance was bound up in coercion and manipulation? What can we say to the generation of girls who go off to school—to learn, to grow, to be enthralled by education and possibility—and are assaulted, raped, by their peers, and denied any justice by their schools' administrative culture?

I sat at dinner discussing a *New York Times* story about sexual assault on college campuses[2] with my parents some time ago, and we wondered if things had always been like this. Did pairs of men use to simply take it upon themselves to penetrate young women on pool tables with a host of objects? Did they, as in an article from earlier that spring,[3] use to lie next to women they'd had sex with in the past, and if she declined their advances on this occasion, just take off her clothes and rape her anyway? Did that happen as frequently in the seventies, when my parents were in college, or fifteen years ago, when I was? Certainly marital rape has a distressingly long history (Renita Weems writes of its biblical precedents in *Battered Love: Marriage, Sex, and Violence in the Hebrew Prophets*[4]), but there was a period in which the culture of sex prior to marriage, among college students at any rate, wasn't structured in quite the same way. Is the frequency of this sort of assault changing, or just the way we talk about it? Are we simply more aware of it now?

I asked my survey respondents if they had any history of sexual abuse, as a victim/survivor or as an abuser. So many said yes, they had been victimized. Roughly a third said yes, a percentage that reflects the results of larger, more rigorously analytical data sets. But one of the benefits of an open response survey like mine is that I can see responses like this:

Do you have any history of sexual abuse?
"No."

But she continues:

> I once slept with a guy when I was blacked out drunk who I believe was either not at all drunk or was sober enough to know that I had blacked out. I don't consider it a rape, though it's possible someone else would feel that it was.

Semantics matter: I don't want to tell someone she's framing her story wrong; but if I were called to testify in a court of law, I'd suggest that the clearly unequal power dynamic in the interaction she describes does not meet the criteria of consensual sex.

Semantics matter, and so do our various interpretations of how to deal with conflict. The article from earlier that spring focused on Swarthmore College, a liberal school outside Philadelphia with a progressive Quaker heritage. That heritage has really only two remaining vestiges today:

The second central remnant of the school's Quaker legacy—the "peaceful resolution of conflicts"—resides not in the student body, but in the administration. "From the very smallest scale to the largest scale, the college does have a long history of finding a way through that won't leave half the people in any room feeling like they lost," says Swarthmore history professor Tim Burke.[5]

I believe in the peaceful resolution of conflicts, of trying to find a way through that doesn't leave anyone out. One problem of that approach, Burke notes, is that "it means . . . we tend to defer difficult decisions." In situations of sexual assault, a larger problem is that it treats perpetrator and victim as equal partners in a conversation: it ignores the problem of power, and more often than not re-victimizes those who have already suffered. The school doesn't want anyone to feel like he's lost, but in some situations, that's not possible. In criminal situations, for example, like this one, that's not possible.

That doesn't mean we can't long and work for restorative justice, but there can never be justice at all if it is the victim whose needs and safety are sacrificed for a veneer of reconciliation.

THIS ALL GOES to say that the injustices of our world are not going to fade away because of the inevitability of increasing goodwill. What liberal Christians mean when we speak of original sin is just this: it's part of our makeup to be estranged from self, God, and neighbor. Existentialist theologians call this the "ambiguity of existence," which means that sometimes good things are good, and sometimes good things have lousy effects. Witness the desire for peaceful reconciliation that hurts the vulnerable. Sometimes lousy things have okay or even good effects. My go-to example is the number of happily married couples I know who initially hooked up at a party; a willingness to pursue casual sexual interaction *need not* end in criminal sexual assault. Sometimes it can be intimate, fun, and even healing or liberating, if my anonymous survey respondents are telling the truth about their experiences.

The ambiguous realm we live in, in which good is sometimes good and sometimes less than fantastic, is referred to in ancient Greek as "*chronos*." But Christians describe another sort of time, "*kairos*," as well. *Kairos* is time outside of time, time in which everything happens, in which all reality is held together. It's the time in which God is: our shorthand has become "God's time," but I kind of loathe that translation, because it gets used far too often to encourage people to sit still and be patient with their suffering. The long single. The marginalized. The victimized. Your intended mate and the justice you seek will come in "God's time." Or never. "In [God's] perspective a thousand years are like yesterday past," Psalm 90:4 says. Best to get comfortable. (This is why Martin Luther King, Jr., had to write "Letter from a Birmingham Jail" and *Why We Can't Wait*.)

"*Kairos*," I think, is better translated as "the eternal": that which is as it was in the beginning, is now, and ever shall be. There are moments, theologians say, when the Eternal One, when God, breaks into *chronos*. The key example of this, the clear, unambiguous example, is in the life, death, and resurrection of Jesus. He ate and slept and hung out and worked within *chronos,* but he also healed, taught, and bore witness to the Good News (*kairos*). He was the eternal within our world: God incarnate.

But just because God's grace—God's eternal love, God's healing presence—was most present in the relatively short thirty-three-year window of Jesus's life doesn't mean that it is never again present. We have a tendency to divide time into before and after God was present in our lives, before and after our conversion, but God breaks into our lives and world regularly. Part of faith is trusting that such a healing presence will show up; part of grace is being able to trust that God will keep working in us and in our world, and subsequently being opened to that healing and reconciliation.

Chronos is ambiguous, sometimes good, sometimes bad, sometimes neither; *kairos,* as we experience it, is fleeting, but persistent; its goodness is unambiguous. Life continues, but God is present. This has important implications for all of us, with our histories, living in the world.

John Wesley, eighteenth-century theologian and revivalist, wrote that God is at work at us "from the first dawning of grace in the soul till it is consummated in glory."

> If we take this in its utmost extent it will include all that is wrought in the soul by what is frequently termed "natural conscience," . . . all the desires after God . . . [through which God is] *showing* every man "to do justly, to love mercy, and to walk humbly with his God;" all the *convictions* which

his Spirit from time to time works in every child
of man.[6]

We can recognize, through this natural conscience, when
something is not right. The women and men who experienced abuse as children and adolescents and into young
adulthood may not have needed anyone to tell them that the
way they were treated was wrong. There's grace in that. We
can't right injustices if we can't first name them.

There's also grace in the assurance that we can trust our
interpretations of what has happened in our lives, even in
the midst of our ambiguous existence.

In *See Me Naked: Stories of Sexual Exile in American
Christianity*, Amy Frykholm writes of Sarah, a young Korean-
American woman wrestling with what it means to be a loving daughter, an American teenager, and an independent but
grounded young woman. She gets a job at the mall. There, a
boy she's not particularly attracted to shows interest. They
go on some dates, during which "she always felt they were
playacting, imagining what other people did or said on dates
and awkwardly trying to do the same."[7]

Her parents go out of town for the weekend, and she
invites him over, without really knowing why—perhaps because this is what teenagers do? She shows him her room,
she sits with him on the bed, and then "he had sex with
[her], and [she] let him."[8] Afterward, she feels terrible. She
showers a bunch of times. She cannot believe she gave away
something that is supposed to be sacred.

After reflection, however, Sarah realizes two things. First,
that sex with this boy created a breach with her parents: a

breach she had needed as she began working out her identity independent from, but related to, them. The second is a
painful realization:

> As much as having sex with Jacob had been a ter-
> rible mistake, and as much as she regretted it, it
> had ended something in Sarah that needed ending.
> As soon as it was over, she had awakened to a truer
> self than the one who had gone out with Jacob in
> the first place . . . Why she always had to do the
> wrong thing first in order to learn it was wrong,
> she didn't know . . . It was a lesson that had to be
> lived, however unpleasant.[9]

My hope is that young women and men have the resources they need to avoid learning lessons the hard way,
but I also want us all to be reassured that there's no such
thing as a perfect life lived with no hard lessons. A young
clergywoman I met at a conference recently told me that
she'd grown up in a conservative Christian culture that insisted that all sex outside marriage was sinful, so she and
her boyfriend had waited. They'd started dating at eighteen,
married five years later, and had waited to share physical
intimacy, even as they grew in love for each other. They've
been married more than a decade, and she told me that
though she is tremendously happy in her marriage, she re-
grets that they missed out on all those years together of hot,
late-adolescent sexual discovery. "I feel like I was sold a bill
of goods," she said, "and that instead I just missed five years
when I could have been enjoying sex with a loving partner."

Her regret can be read as a hard lesson, but a *kairos* moment nonetheless, in that it led her to a deeper exploring of Christian norms and teachings, and that critical exploration in turn sparked her passion for ministry.

Sarah, the young woman in Frykholm's book, gets to college and discovers what her afternoon tryst with Jacob has taught her:

> not how to be more like her peers, but how to be more like herself. The questions raised by that encounter were still burning. . . . In her haste to detach sex and herself from its oppressive cultural, religious, and familial meanings, [Sarah] plunged herself deep into the wilderness, a place in which her life experience has only grown richer, more complex, where her questions daily grow less easy to answer.[10]

Our lives, our existence, our day-to-day time, are ambiguous, and can feel like a wilderness. Though we often experience ambiguity or even ambivalence about some of our choices and the events of our lives within that wilderness, our time there, like Sarah's, can be rich and even include *kairos* moments, glimpses of grace. There is no brokenness, no sin—of our own or committed against us—that can define us. We may be thrust into the wilderness, we may be shaped indefinitely by it, but there is no telling what God will make with us during our time within its darkness and light. Indeed, it's often within the wilderness that we come to know ourselves to be saved.

What is salvation? John Wesley asks.

It is not the soul's going to heaven . . . it is not a
blessing which lies on the other side of death, or
(as we usually speak) in the other world. The very
words of the text [Ephesians 2:8, KJV] itself put this
beyond all question. "Ye *are* saved." It is not something at a distance: it is a present thing, a blessing
which, through the free mercy of God, ye are now
in possession of.[11]

Salvation, then, isn't something we wait or long for; it's
something that's being worked in our lives even now, the
kairos interrupting the *chronos*. It begins to work in us in that
natural conscience, in that *prevenient grace,*[12] until we reach
the moment of greatest clarification: that we are children of
God, living in a broken world, usually at odds with ourselves
and others, but nonetheless, all at once, also loved beyond
measure and being drawn into reconciliation and holiness.
We are *pardoned,* the historic language goes. We are not in
this wilderness alone. A turning point in Sarah's story is
when she, who has held the story of sex with Jacob close
to her, in secret and in shame, shares it with a friend, who
in turn "holds it gently."[13] Sarah's realization that she is not
alone changes her. Whether it's the love of Christ manifest in
a friend or the assurance of Christ's own presence, this *jus-
tifying* grace brings a sense of peace. Even when I look back
at my own story, with the boyfriend who returned my sock
in the chapel, experiences of *kairos* have transformed the
effects of my *chronos* memories, to the point at which I can
share the story, laughing in empathy with my former self
and a grad student smarting from a recent breakup.

Claiming a life with God, following Jesus, is, I hope it's clear, neither about throwing our hands in the air and accepting ambivalence as a vision for life, nor about writing off what has come before as sinful and irredeemable. I recently baptized two adult women who came to Christianity out of another tradition. As we walked through the liturgy, I was very clear that when I would ask each of them if they renounced the spiritual forces of wickedness and repented of their sin, that wasn't to say their lives before were particularly sinful, or that their prior tradition was a spiritual force of wickedness. Rather, baptism is an outward sign of this experience of justification; an acknowledgment that while we live an ambiguous existence, we are accepting the divine invitation to be moved ever more closely into the divine life, the *kairos* moments in the midst of our day-to-day.

WHEN JOSH AND I were planning our wedding, we asked my friend Sandhya Jha (a multitalented pastor, writer, and activist, and the same friend who suggested I listen to David Gray's song on repeat while writing chapter four) to sing in the service. She agreed, and then the hard work began: finding a theologically appropriate song for a wedding. Something about romantic love, and the holy within it; the feeling of finding the one with whom you could promise to build a life, with whom you were willing to take this leap of faith. One floated option was "First Day of My Life" by Bright Eyes: *Yours is the first face that I saw / I think I was blind before I met you.* Another was "Don't Let Us Get Sick," a Warren Zevon tune: *Don't let us get sick / Don't let us get old / Don't let us get stupid, all right?*

Our pastor vetoed these: "You don't want to say that; you've both been in love before; those experiences shaped you. You don't want to pray that bad things won't happen; they will. You want to ask for the sustaining grace to stay together through all the things, good and bad."

In the end, Sandhya wrote us a song, because her multi-talented nature wasn't obvious enough already: *Everything in life takes some risk,* the chorus proclaimed.

We need courage to take the risk of building intimacy with other people, we need courage, too, to look clear-eyed (bright-eyed?) at our past and interpret it. People regularly try to simply push hard memories aside; the harder the memories, the less I blame them. Survivors of sexual violence experience panic attacks at higher rates than normal, and sometimes exhibit symptoms of post-traumatic stress disorder. If their families, or communities, or institutions do not provide the support needed to clean out their emotional wounds, they may well have those wounds close up, harboring an infection inside that can fester and cause additional pain. It stings to clean a wound, to poke it and prod it until certain that any contagions have been excised, but we want to heal.

Healing requires courage, especially if it means reopening old wounds. If those old wounds include sins wrought by others—sins both criminal and mundane—part of healing may bring about accusation or conflict, something that could be even more traumatizing.

There's no short road to healing. Wesley noted that having experienced justification by no means ensures that we now live in constant peace, tranquillity, and joy. Nor does it inure us to further suffering or prevent us from committing further sin. But:

> At the same time that we are justified, yea, in that very moment sanctification begins. . . . We are . . . born of the Spirit. There is a *real* as well as a *relative* change. We are inwardly renewed by the power of God. . . .
> Temptations return and sin revives, showing it was but stunned before, not dead.[14]

We feel two forces within us—sin and temptation, brokenness and endless aching; and the grace and love of God. But there is good news: "they find one or more of these [hurts and sins] frequently stirring in their heart, though not *conquering.*"[15]

The grace of God, the *kairos* moments of realization, is present throughout our lives, but after the first moment of assurance, that grace strengthens and empowers us to live more fully in love. That love enables us to remember the grace and steadfast love present in our histories, and to gain critical distance and, we hope, healing from the brokenness we may have known.

As we grow more perfect in love—that is, as God's sanctifying grace grows in us—that work, or healing and healthy distancing, grows easier. As that work grows in magnitude, we may be more able to seek justice where it is needed and to hold lightly the ambiguities of our past.

Memory is a funny thing. Sometimes it haunts us; sometimes it reminds us happily of who we've been and from whence we've come. William Faulkner once famously wrote, "The past is never dead. It isn't even past," and he's got a point. The mistakes, the hurts, the joys of what has come before all linger, and they affect the present in incalculable ways. But. With grace, with reflection, with the quest for healing and the experience of salvation, the past's influence can wane. Only if we attend to it will this happen. But as it does, we may find that we are ever more able to be present in this moment and its relationships.

I love "Amazing Grace"; I know it by heart. However, it's not the oft-quoted first verse that makes me cry; it's this one:

> Through many dangers, toils and snares,
> I have already come;
> 'Tis grace hath brought me safe thus far,
> And grace will lead me home.

Chapter Eight

Be Faithful

A Theology of Fidelity

W hen I danced the night away with my "London friend,"
with his hand on my waist and my heart pounding
in my chest, the night my appreciation for "Blurred
Lines" was preemptively forged, I was dating someone else.

My boyfriend, the one who had kissed me sloppily on
the steps on the way to winning my heart, and I had been
together for a scant four months. I loved him dearly. We
had an agreement, though. I was pretty sure I would marry
him one day (turns out I was wrong), but I was only twenty,
and I wanted to be free to make out with a few strangers in
British pubs if the occasion arose. I didn't want the possibility of such a minor, but (to my mind) quintessential, study

abroad experience to come between us. I didn't want to have to choose between my love and my freedom. Not at twenty. Not if we were going to be together forever starting when I got back stateside.

That agreement proved to be all fine and well and good. I kissed a few strangers. I got to feel desirable and young, stupid and carefree. For a largely responsible oldest child, total nerd, this was an important rite of passage. It proved to be not a particularly big deal; it was within the agreed-upon bounds of our relationship.

The real problem arose when I met someone I was crazy about, another American in the program, who had these eyes and this smile, and who introduced me to *Bird by Bird*, Anne Lamott's great writing book. We were friends, but we had chemistry. We walked home from class and shared shortcuts through the tony alleys of South Kensington; we talked about books. We saw plays for five pounds sterling, ate at awesome restaurants, and danced away Wednesday nights in the cheesy Covent Garden club that featured one-pound drink specials. We were almost always in groups. He was dating a statuesque Ivy Leaguer. I was in love with someone else.

This other boy, he of the writing classes and the nights dancing, was also technically allowed by his girlfriend to make out with strangers in bars. Still, nothing ever happened between us. Just lots of fraught silences and loaded looks. Now it's possible, certainly, that this boy was never interested in me as anything more than a friend—I am well versed in unrequited crushes, and projecting content onto awkward silences—but I know I was scared that if I pursued anything with this boy, I would have to end things with my beloved back home.

A kiss in a bar is one thing; an emotional connection over books and vocation is quite another.

I didn't, back then, quite understand how fidelity worked. I figured as long as we weren't making out, I wasn't breaking any promises. It was okay for me to dream about this other boy, to write letters and e-mails, to invite him to visit when we got back to the States, because "nothing ever happened." I hadn't ever kissed him—though I'd sure as hell thought about it—so I was, technically, being faithful. I thought the "technically" part mattered.

Nearly fifteen years later, I encountered a man who bears a physical resemblance to that boy. Not the Boyfriend, the Other One. The nose is different; this guy is taller. We are acquaintances, but one morning it struck me that he looked like my old crush. I'd never noticed it before because we are both parents and know each other only in the context of our children; I do not connect my children with old flames. The resemblance hit me one morning when this dad made a passing comment to me and I felt a flush rise in my cheeks, when I became aware, in a day care parking lot, of the blood rushing south, pounding through my abdomen.

It was weird. Also fleeting. I didn't think about it again until I came home to work on this chapter. But having that feeling, the rush of attraction and arousal, made me contemplative.

Was this feeling a challenge to my faithfulness to my beloved husband?

Which made me wonder: What do we do with fidelity?

★ good fidelity question

Most people would probably say this is an important part of a relationship; however, both church and culture struggle to interpret fidelity in relationships in the sort of robust ways that will help people to actually be faithful. Rather than a romantic, and usually incorrect, notion that fidelity means never again feeling the rush of attraction, or shutting down the part of your brain that notices lovely strangers, a Christian sense of fidelity is one grounded in mutual promise and the hope of a shared life.

MUCH AS MARRIAGE used to be understood as a clear boundary outside of which sex was not supposed to (properly) occur, fidelity in a relationship used to be pretty generally understood to mean "not making out with other people." And, if that's the criterion we're still using, I was probably solidly within the bounds of fidelity in both of the above instances.

I'm not sure, however, that "refraining from engaging in sexual activities with someone who is not your partner" is a sufficient definition of fidelity. Neither does the imperative "don't cheat" capture the spirit of faithfulness. Maybe because you expect a positive definition of something that is supposed to be full of faith, not just a list of things to avoid.

One of these experiences, though, was out of my mind and off my conscience within three and a half minutes, while the other has become a source of some regret (and book fodder) years later. What was the difference?

There was a time when my fairly ridiculous reaction to a personable, benign comment from an acquaintance would have undone me completely. I had carried some certainty into my marriage with Josh because during the two years as a couple prior to our wedding, I'd never looked askance. Those two years marked the beginning of the longest period of fidelity I'd ever experienced; ours was the first relationship in which I could consider a long lifetime of monogamy as both romantic and possible, as opposed to frightening. We'd had a passionate beginning and our intimate bond was easily wrought.

Those years at the beginning of a relationship, of easy devotion and delicious infatuation, slowly melt into years in which devotion and infatuation, in which passion and desire, can and should yet exist; but the pastoral care literature—the stuff pastors are supposed to use to instruct young couples—carefully warns that those lovesick feelings of contentment no longer come so effortlessly. Desire has to be kindled, hearts have to be guarded against encroaching feelings, devotion requires intention. If feelings arise for others, it's because something's going on in your marriage.

I love to study theology, a discipline concerned with symbols, and relationships, and making meaning of our experiences in the world. My job—teaching, writing, preaching, providing pastoral care—requires that I pay attention to the meaning we make of our lives: thus, in my book, everything means something. But what I've learned over time is that not everything means what I think it means. Sometimes, people interpret things incorrectly.

Part of the difficulty arises from the fact that most of us are operating under a couple of different understandings of the nature of fidelity in any given moment. We may use contractual language: we have agreed to be monogamous, and thus cheating is breaking the contract. Anything short of cheating, though, is fine. Others of us hold a romantic vision of love as the fulfillment of all our desires in our partner, in which any desire for any other person is a betrayal. In our wedding, as in many, the pastor prayed, "What God has joined together, let no one break asunder," and Josh and I vowed to "forsake all others and be faithful" to each other as long as we both shall live. Those promises, though, had been present, and largely explicit, for Josh and me long before the hot July day on which we wed.

Just about every couple I've ever worked with as they prepare to get married is totally on board with forsaking all others, in theory. I know far more romantics than contract negotiators. We grew up on *Romeo and Juliet:* stories of love blooming against all odds, of lovers preferring to die than be apart. The church plays into this, too, with discussion of mutual self-sacrifice and service and viral blog posts about how love and marriage are not *for you.* (Hint: they're apparently for your partner.)[1]

It's not that Christians are generating those narratives ex nihilo. A number of New Testament epistles are routinely read as advice guides for healthy, faithful relationships. But the one that seems to incontrovertibly convict anyone who's ever so much as thrilled to the presence of an attractive stranger on the train comes from the mouth of Jesus himself.

> "You have heard that it was said, 'You shall not commit adultery.' But I say to you that everyone who looks at a woman with lust has already committed adultery with her in his heart."
>
> (MATTHEW 5:27–28)

where does the sin occur

Jesus is (perhaps unsurprisingly) right: you don't need to actually commit adultery to have sinned against your partner (and probably yourself and God, too). But desire isn't exactly the same as lust, even if it's for someone to whom you're not currently bound in a covenant relationship.

The recent morning on which I felt a flush of desire wasn't so much my body longing for anything or anyone in particular, but might have been a signal of any number of things. The curious way sensory memory works, given this guy's resemblance to that long-ago boy. Or maybe that I was ovulating, given that just about everything gets me going when I'm ovulating. Or, most likely, the flush of desire may have been related to the fact that I am writing a book about sex. These thoughts and feelings are rather close to the surface for me right now.

At any rate, when I got home, ready to write, I checked my calendar against the ovulation theory, and then let the feeling go, not just from my body, but from my mind. And thus I don't think that moment constituted adultery, or even lust.

Some definitions might be in order.

WHETHER IT STARTS in late childhood or early adolescence, or doesn't make an appearance until we're older, at some point we realize that we are more attracted to some people than others. Physically attracted—we like their eyes or hair or build, or just the general look of them—or attracted to another attribute: the sound of their voice or the way they tell stories, their worldview or compassion. The nature of *attraction* can reveal as much about us as about the other person; it tells us about our preferences, whether momentary or persisting, about our mood and our perceived needs.

What I'd call *chemistry* (not in the sense of stoichiometry and pipettes and acids and bases that can burn a hole in your shirt if you're not paying attention) can develop when there's a mutual attraction; it's the charge, the spark that seems to pull two people together. It exists in the give and take of conversation, in the pull that draws you to stand ever closer to the other person. I'm not great on etymology, but I think it's called chemistry because two people, thrown together, make something new: they create something—energy, maybe, but sometimes something more. There is the possibility of burning a hole in something. There's sexual chemistry, of course, but there are other types, too: the way good friends play off each other, or colleagues on a project, or a writer with her editor. Madeleine L'Engle, married for decades and writer for even longer, describes this beautifully:

> A true friendship has become more and more a lost art in a society which feels that in order for a relationship to be fulfilled it must end in bed. A true friendship is always amoureuse; it is part of my human sexuality; each encounter with a friend is a time of creation . . . My relationship with my editor has got to be amourous. This doesn't mean sexual indulgence . . . It does mean something is happening on that non-empirical level, in the mediating band between nightside and sunside. . . . Many editors are qualified . . . But with only a few is the spark set off in me, so that I know what must be done to make a manuscript come alive.[2]

★ question abt chemistry & physicality

There's a decisively physical element to much of what we think of as chemistry, which is part of what makes it exciting, and part of what makes it risky. It's why dancing can be foreplay; a pair can test out how easily and unconsciously they can get their bodies to move together in rhythm. Josh and I had been married for maybe five years when we stood on a North Carolina beach and shared one of the hottest moments of our relationship, in plain sight of my extended family. We threw a ball back and forth, back and forth. Sometimes it landed right in my hand; sometimes, our limbs lengthened to grab it from the air just above our heads. Watching him stretch, his grace and strength, feeling my own arms and legs moving to meet his throw, I wanted him. I delighted in the cadence of our dance, and gave thanks that no one in my family reads minds. A Nerf football has never been so sexy.

One of the reasons I married Josh is because we have chemistry six ways from Sunday: we dance well together physically and metaphorically. But while he's the only person with whom I share chemistry on all those levels, I still manage to connect with other people on a host of other levels. Josh is my only husband, my only lover, my best friend: but he is not the only person I know and love.

Esther Perel, a couples and family therapist, muses: chemistry w/ others?

We all share a fundamental need for security, which propels us toward committed relationships in the first place; but we have an equally strong need for adventure and excitement. Modern romance promises that it's possible to meet these two distinct sets of needs in one place. Still, I'm not convinced. Today, we turn to one person to provide what an entire village once did: a sense of grounding, meaning, and continuity. At the same time, we expect our committed relationships to be romantic as well as emotionally and sexually fulfilling.[3]

Just as Josh is not particularly interested in the ins and outs of denominational politics nor of theological arguments, I can't keep track of the personalities and challenges of the eighty or so students he teaches *each year*. I'm good with names and faces, but he is forever being greeted in our town, at the library, in the grocery store, by students current and former, whom I have never heard of nor seen before. After years in this school district, there are literally hundreds of them.

I can't be jealous, then, of the fact that he and his colleagues support one another tremendously and want to spend time with one another outside of work: the guys go camping annually; he lunches with the ladies on his team each Friday. For my part, I have worked hard to cultivate an ever-expanding network of awesome colleagues in my own field.

As L'Engle suggests, though, the question is not whether there's something lacking in our spouse that makes us want to have more than one friendship or relationship in our lives—but whether those other relationships support us individually and as a couple in healthy ways. I'm invited to lunch with the ladies and Josh; he's welcome to talk church

key!

nerd whenever he wants; his colleagues and mine value our marriage and are rooting for it.

So, too, do we rely on siblings and friends and parents to enliven and enrich our lives. Jesus said, "The thief comes only to steal and kill and destroy. I came that they may have life, and have it abundantly" (John 10:10). Jealousy, possessiveness, a need to be the only relationship in a partner's life—those are thieves that steal, kill, and destroy. A community that provides grounding, meaning, connection, and joy is a critical contribution to the abundant life Jesus describes. But so are fidelity and trust within our *primary relationship*.

Attraction is not always sexual, and tells us as much about ourselves as anyone else; chemistry is mutual and not always sexual, but usually awesome, as long as it supports your primary relationship. *Arousal* is the sexual side of attraction and, similarly, tells us as much about ourselves as anyone else. But it's not always another person, or something they're doing or saying, that gets us hot and bothered. I could smell Josh's deodorant out in the world and be ready to go most of the time, hear a certain song and be filled with longing, either because it calls up a memory or simply because it's full of poetry.

For a long time, I thought that being in love with one person meant only having eyes for them. (*Shbop-shbop.*) That's how you know, right? When you can't think of anyone else, when she's on your mind all the time: his smile, her voice, the way he makes you laugh, the way she sees you. My college boyfriend was the one I loved, and then I met someone else who made me feel that way. With whom I wanted to spend as much time as I could; with whom I felt alive. Not more alive than when I was with my boyfriend, but *also* alive.

A therapist friend and I were talking about couples the other day. I usually see them before they're married; she sees them after. When I see them, when they are planning their weddings, they are usually still delightfully infatuated. By the time she does, they are no longer in that space wherein they crave each other without thinking, wherein they are barreling toward each other in the hope of ecstatic reunion. Their intimate familiarity has grown, and their all-consuming desire has cooled.

Perel suggests that this cooling has more to do with the paradoxical nature of intimacy and desire than it does with the relative health of anyone's particular relationship. In our lasting relationships, we want closeness, and stability. We experience change as stressful and threatening to the life we've built together. But desire, the erotic, the singular focus on our partner and the thrilling feeling of butterflies in our stomachs, sweaty palms, and breathless anticipation: those things require uncertainty, and distance. Not grave, unconquerable distance, but some. How can you breathlessly anticipate the arrival of your lover, when most of the time the greatest distance between you is between two apartments, or (worse!) the kitchen and the bathroom? In a deeply intimate relationship, you *share* a lot. The erotic asks for concealment, negotiating, back-and-forth.

Perel's wondrous reminder, the one that my therapist friend and I realized in our discussion, is that people think it's right, good, and necessary to trade one feeling for the other. *It is worth it,* people say, committing to monogamy;

are intimacy the erotic mutually exclusive

intimacy is worth the decline of the erotic. This is what growing up is all about. But they're wrong.

We should never sacrifice one fundamental need for another, and we're fooling ourselves if we think we can.

We need both; Jesus did not come to rob our lives of richness, but to help us live into life's fullness. Jesus would not encourage us in an attempt to kill some vital force within us; we're supposed to notice beauty in the world, the amazing individuality of every living person. As L'Engle says, "If our love for each other really is participatory, then all other human relationships nourish it; it is inclusive, never exclusive."[4] We're supposed to relish the ties that bind us to one another and the creative energy that flows among us. Jesus surely appreciates my freckles and sense of humor, and Josh's way with words and the way he slips into "Dance-y Hammond" mode if we stay at a party for long enough. If God cares about the sparrows, and counts each and every hair on our heads, surely we are following in the spirit of Christ when we notice the generous way she is with kids, or the length of her calf; when we *see* his concern for his justice, and the way he fills out his shirt.

That said, as Paul reminds us, always: "Everything is permitted, but everything isn't beneficial. Everything is permitted, but everything doesn't build others up" (1 Corinthians 10:23, CEB). Depending on whether he or she or we are single, if there's any disproportionate power relationship dynamic between us, if we have the sort of rapport that warrants the giving of compliments, it may not be beneficial, appropriate, to give voice to the fine qualities we've noticed in another. It may not even be beneficial or appropriate to entertain ongoing thoughts about the lovely attributes so-and-so has going for them.

W HEN J ESUS WARNS the gathered people about adultery and lust, he does some more scriptural interpretive work: "You have heard that it was said, 'Don't commit adultery.' But I say to you that every man who looks at a woman lustfully has already committed adultery in his heart" (Matthew 5:27–28, CEB).

Good old Jesus, raising the stakes. The commandment from Sinai prohibits adultery. *Thou shalt not . . .* But Jesus suggests that it's not just our actions that can cause harm. You don't have to follow through; you just have to think about it.

Surely that's a metaphor, right? It isn't really *just as bad* to cheat than to sort of contemplate it, is it? What's the difference between appreciating someone's God-given hotness and lusting after them sinfully?

Some Christians[5] define lust as thinking or doing anything sexual without your spouse, including but not limited to teenage masturbatory fantasy, a little bit of imagination about an ex or a celebrity, and desiring someone. I think that's drawing the circle a little wide. How, after all, do you find the person you want to make your spouse without experiencing a bit of sexual desire?

Rather, the sticking point for me is the object of the desire. For those Christians just mentioned, any object other than a spouse is a problem. But if we don't believe that all pleasure, all desire for unmarried folks is necessarily wrong, that's an insufficient definition. Philosopher Simon Blackburn comes closer to the point: "Love is individual: there is only the unique Other, the doted upon, the single star around whom the lover revolves. Lust takes what comes."[6]

The question of lust isn't necessarily just one of monogamy, then—it's about the failure to value someone for who they are, in the fullness of their humanity. Margaret Farley writes,

> As we frequently understand it, lust is a craving for sexual pleasure without any real affective response to, union with, or affirmation of the other. If there is any love here, it is of oneself, for the sake of which something or someone else is "lusted after." The objects of lust are in this sense fungible, they are whatever entices one in sexually passionate ways.[7]

Blackburn and Farley lead us toward a definition: lust is sinful because it devalues others as individuals. Lust isn't really concerned with the particulars of another, about his body or her interest or her consent.

A lusting suitor might deny this charge, caring mightily, even obsessively, about the particular characteristics of the object of his desire. What moves desire into the realm of lust? Or burning, fiery, passionate longing into excess?

If love is about valuing another and honoring God's image within her, lust is *less* concerned with the good of the other than with the meeting of a desire for union. It's not that no affection for the object exists, just that his needs and wants are not the priority.

Lust is sinful because it fails the test of neighbor love . . . but it can also fail the test of self-love, too. Blackburn writes, "When we talk of lust it might seem clear enough what we are talking about: sexual desire . . . But that does not get to the heart of it."[8] There is something about lust that is inherently selfish, but selfishness is not the same as the self-love to which God calls us. The sin of gluttony works as a less-politicized analogy: the glutton eats and eats, depriving others of food they need, not caring for their lack; but eating like that will kill a body before too long.

Lust dismisses the needs of others, but also tends to evidence a willful ignorance of its possessor's own needs. Lust is about sexual desire, but it's usually about something else, too. Heck, even sexual desire itself is usually about more than one thing, too; human beings are complicated.

Poet Marc O'Brien contracted polio at the age of six, and spent the rest of his life in an iron lung, profoundly physically disabled. In 1990, he wrote a story for *The Sun* about his quest to understand his sexuality as a person with a disability, and his strong desire to experience sexual touch and intimacy with another person. His essay, "On Seeing a Sex Surrogate," was made into a 2012 movie starring Helen Hunt, and both renderings of the story are helpful in parsing the complexity of human desire. "It took me years to discover that what separated me from [others] was fear—fear of others, fear of making decisions, fear of my own sexuality, and a surpassing dread of my parents."[9]

Growing into adulthood requires—for all of us—finding the courage to reach out to others, and to embrace our sexuality as a source of vitality instead of shame. O'Brien writes:

As a man in my thirties, I still felt embarrassed by
my sexuality. It seemed to be utterly without purpose in my life, except to mortify me when I became aroused during bed baths. I would not talk to
my attendants about the orgasms I had then, or the
profound shame I felt. I imagined they, too, hated
me for becoming so excited.

O'Brien experienced his body as a betrayer: not entirely outside himself—for he felt as emotionally passive as
physically—but working against his best interest.

I wanted to be loved. I wanted to be held, caressed,
and valued. But my self-hatred and fear were too
intense.[10]

In O'Brien's testimony, his sexual desires and impulses are
solitary; though he longed to be in love, to have a sexual relationship with a beloved, he had emotional work of his own to
do before he could pursue such a thing. But the focus of his
desires on sexual acts, and on his own needs, is not sinful.
Neither, I'd argue, is the important work done by Cheryl, the
sex surrogate, or the advice given by Father Mike, the local
Catholic priest, who suggests: "Jesus was never big on rules,
and he often broke the rules out of compassion."[11]

O'Brien's story compels because it raises complex questions and reminds us again that sexual desire is not in and
of itself the same thing as lust; what moves me is his un-
flinching commitment to self-examination. More often than
not, those in the throes of lust aren't able to be honest with

themselves about what they really desire. Sex, maybe. But also affirmation of a sort; or connection, or a thrill. Maybe an escape. Sometimes sex is an easy way to avoid harder conversations. A number of my survey respondents reported in retrospect using sexual activity with someone other than their partner in early relationships to provoke jealousy or a breakup they couldn't otherwise imagine initiating.

On the flip side of lust—whether that sin lies in thought or action—lies faithfulness: to God, to our partners, and to ourselves. Faithfulness doesn't require so much the policing of our thoughts, an anxious attention to propriety, but a living into the fullness of our promises and relationships.

When I met the fellow journalism student in London, I wasn't blindly lusting. In fact, in the context of my relationship, passing lust worked out on Australians with work visas at our local pub was preferable (if less ethical according to the norms of chapter three) to actually *caring* for someone else. But my growing feelings for my friend challenged my faithfulness, because I started imagining what it would be like to be with him *instead of* my boyfriend. I hedged my bets on the future of my committed relationship, loitered near the metaphorical doorway with one foot outside it.

I've wondered on occasion what made it so hard for me to get my head around what was going on; why I couldn't see my faithlessness for what it was. I believed in fidelity. I'd been surrounded by models of it. But I hadn't realized that you could feel love for more than one person at once.

We're called to a life of abundant love, to connection with lots of people. To our parents and siblings, friends and

strangers. We're called to see the best in people, to appreciate and value them in their fullness. I shouldn't have been
surprised that in the midst of trying to love my neighbor, I
might, you know, start to feel *love* for my neighbor. It's possible, it turns out, that you can be attracted to more than one
person, even more than one person at one time. But it's not
possible to grow into the abundance of love, to grow more
perfect in love, if you're hedging your bets.

The myth of "the One" is powerful in our culture, and I
object to it for how much harder it can make life for single
folks, but it also presents a challenge to fidelity. The idea
that we are each intended for just one person has led more
than one person in a committed relationship to wonder if
they have been in error making a commitment to their partner, if they are instead *supposed* to be with the person awakening new (or old, or faded) feelings in them.

Instead of measuring potential suitors against the imagined criteria of the One, we might be better served by considering Christian practices of discernment. The Quaker
tradition uses the language of "way open" or "way closed."
God's grace and the Holy Spirit move in us and in the world.
Sometimes doors open and that opening allows us to see a
way forward in a decision. Sam loved Chris, but they were
from different parts of the country, and it was vitally important to each of them that they eventually settle in the
vicinity of their families of origin. Neither could imagine
compromising. Their love was good and strong, but this
unbridgeable conflict seemed like a door closing on their
relationship. Adam loved Amanda, but he wanted kids and
she didn't. If they'd decided to stay together, his becoming a

father would be a way closed to him, but he'd have the open door of a life with someone he loved.

When you make a promise to be faithful to one person, that means that you're intentionally closing the door to certain types of relationships with other people. Those relationships might have been wonderful. You might have made a life with someone different from your spouse. But you didn't. You chose one way and not another.

Our culture has for a long time spoken of the way of marriage and commitment as not simply a door, but a cage. The title of Esther Perel's book, *Mating in Captivity,* comes from a D. H. Lawrence poem, "Wild Things in Captivity":

> The great cage of our domesticity
> kills sex in a man, the simplicity
> of desire is distorted and twisted awry.[12]

Perel's description of the paradox of needs in a long relationship is a useful rejoinder to that way of thinking. We long for commitment, for security and intimacy, but we will, mostly, if we're not experiencing depression or low levels of vitamin D or testosterone, not cease to desire the thrills of an erotic life simply because we've made a commitment.

Lawrence's last stanza offers a solution:

> Sex is a state of grace.
> In a cage it can't take place.
> Break the cage, then, start in and try.[13]

Perel rejects the solution, and the reasoning, that if you want to have sex, you have to break the cage of marriage. So do I. It's true that sex is a state of grace, and that it can't exist in all its wonder and glory in captivity. But our culture is wrong in equating commitment with a cage. We walk through the open door into committed relationships, subsequently closing other doors. That door opens up, however, not to a tiny room with too close walls, but into the wild blue yonder.

There is nothing more expansive than the erotic imagination of human beings, Perel suggests. Commitment to one partner can be, should be, an opening to a space wider than our imagining.

The problem of infidelity is a problem of lust—but not because it is an insatiable desire for sex. Rather, infidelity manifests a failure to attend to our needs for recognition and surprise, for self-awareness and desire, within our relationships, instead focusing on someone else. While her particulars may be lovely, she could really be anyone, because the desire for her is about meeting the seeker's needs, not creating a new relationship in love. The problem of infidelity is a problem of lust, because ignoring one's commitments sacrifices the needs of the partner on the altar of the pursuer's greed. If you've promised to forsake all others, it's a sin against your partner to cease forsaking them.

Perel suggests a number of ways to negotiate and be intentional in engaging erotic imagination within committed relationships. But she says that all the tricks and toys and new positions our culture describes in women's and lads' mags are not the important factors. She instructs, "If we are to maintain desire with one person over time we must be able to bring a sense of the unknown into a familiar space. In the words of Proust, 'The real voyage of discovery consists not in seeking new landscapes but in having new eyes.'"[14]

Jesus is forever talking about having eyes to see and ears to hear. Whether it's the reign of God being born among us or the thing that attracted us to our partner in the first place, we need to be intentional in looking for it, in seeing it with new eyes. We assume that when we're in love, the rest will simply fall into place, but, as Perel notes, spontaneity—in sex or in intimacy—is a myth. We have to be intentional.

It can seem like a drag—and indeed, every now and again, it is, even with someone we dearly love; but if the relationship is worth investing in, the investment is worthwhile.

JOSH AND I have been together for over a decade now, and because our relationship is on pretty solid ground, there is less surprise, less intrigue, and virtually no pining in my life. We check in with each other about too much; I never have time to pine. And, should I ever need a fix of those things, of pining and intrigue, I can read, or browse romantic movies on Netflix, or engineer a period of separation from my beloved. (Our third child was totally conceived after Josh had been away at a writing residency for two weeks. This is surely not a coincidence.)

In truth, those easy things are more than sufficient. I was horrible at dating. When I first started up with Josh, I could tell things would be serious (not least because he was best friends with my roommate, and if I screwed up our nascent relationship I'd have to hunt for another apartment). I hadn't been single for terrifically long; as someone well practiced at serial monogamy, I'd been (sort of?) enjoying a period of just going on dates.

I wondered about this to my mother—*Am I ready for this?*— and she said, "Bromleigh, my child, you are no good at being single. You are built for relationships."

I was more than a little surprised to hear this from her (and it must be said that she only said this to me when I was twenty-three, at the age she thought it was well-nigh time for me to be finding a serious partner), but she was totally right.

I find my depression harder to manage when I'm single. When I was dating, pining, obsessing over unreturned phone calls, I didn't get my work done. I spent too much time moping to get my papers written.

I knew my relationship with Josh was different because there was no drama. He made sure that I graduated on time (he selflessly played Madden football on his PlayStation while I read theology and worked out economics problem sets sitting next to him on the couch). There's not a ton of intrigue, because there's too much trust. Our love is the solid ground I stand on. There's not a ton of intrigue, but there's adventure, and the mutual enabling of self-exploration: without his support, I would not have written a sex book; without my encouragement, he would not have pursued a master's degree in a program he loves.

Being faithful in our relationships is sometimes harder than we might have imagined—it simply doesn't come without some effort, not for anybody—but a faithful love is also better than we might ever have imagined. Firmly grounded in a trusting relationship, we know the assurance of grace that enables us to go out into the world and love widely, deeply, and ever more perfectly in love. We can, in Perel's words, "not merely survive, but revive":[15] we can pursue pleasure and connection, creativity and passion. In a faithful relationship, we can stop hedging our bets, and take a leap of faith.

Chapter Nine

The Avoidable and the Inevitable

Theology Around Leaving and Staying

've never been good at identifying when a relationship should rightly have ended. By the time my first love and I broke up for the last time, we'd flickered on and off for years like a slowly dying fluorescent lightbulb. Not that I'm advocating for incandescent breakups. I've been on the receiving end of the quick pop and flash of light before darkness, and I hate that sort of surprise, that sort of pace. But the flickering is terrible in its own way. It's annoying, and while your eyes can adjust (people can adjust to almost anything, after all), you almost inevitably end up with a pounding headache.

Part of my problem used to lie in my inability to discern

the difference between "loving someone" and "being able to build a future with him." Just as I'd grown up bearing witness to the reality of imperfect relationships that nonetheless were fruitful and full of joy and love, I wondered if each entry in my series of imperfect relationships would be the one I'd commit to over time. What are the things you're supposed to compromise on? How do you know if it's time to up the ante or fold?

The great fun of a relationship is the grace it can bring: the sense of having a teammate with whom you can stick it out through thick and thin. Who loves you regardless. Who loves you unconditionally. Who has seen you warts and all, and still wants to be with you.

That grace underlies the wedding vows we all know: "I take you to be mine, for better and worse, for richer and poorer, in sickness and in health, until death do us part." No matter what.

I attended a wedding once where some friends of the couple performed the song "Come What May," from *Moulin Rouge! Seasons may change, winter to spring / But I love you until the end of time.* It was a good pick. Captures the lifelong promise, captures the grace. Whatever happens, I'll love you.

The couple divorced.

I mention this not to pour the salt of irony in devastating wounds—I am not privy to what happened, I only know it was really difficult—but to say that despite our hopes and intentions, sometimes relationships fall apart. Theologian Stanley Hauerwas once wrote that sex should rightly happen only in relationships in which one can imagine a future, but it is so hard to know what the future will hold. Will experiences of hardship and suffering bring partners closer together or drive them apart? Will uncovered and previously unknown preferences prove to be insurmountable? Will addictions or affairs destroy trust? Staying together is hard work, even for those with incredible sexual chemistry and totally compatible personalities and similar beliefs . . . Relationships must be tended, love cultivated. In this chapter, we'll look at the things that can aid those efforts—kindness, attentiveness, care—listen to stories of those who have ended relationships, and hear a word of hope about the power of love.

We cannot know the future, but that's not to say that the making of promises in a marriage isn't important. The promise to stay together, spoken in front of a gathered congregation or in a private moment, is huge. As Dietrich Bonhoeffer, the eminent theologian and leader in the resistance to the Nazis, once wrote, "It is not your love that sustains the marriage, but from now on, the marriage that sustains your love."[1] The promise, the official entanglements and the buy-in of friends and family, provide structures and support we can lean on when things get hard.

nana always says this

When we are fighting, or troubled, or looking askance, we can remember the promises we made, and the memory of the courage it took to make that leap of faith can embolden us to try again, to summon up the strength to be our best selves, to make a better effort. Married couples still fight, and suffer through rough patches, after they've made their vows, but it's both easier to stay together and harder to leave than before those promises are made and the legalities are finalized. Marriage is not a panacea, but it is an institution.

remedy

YET, DESPITE OUR best hopes and the strength of an ancient institution, there are some things that we might consider a bridge too far. Deal breakers. They're different for everybody. Josh has an absolute no-smoking policy. I am incapable of falling in love with someone lacking a sense of humor. My mother has very little patience for inflexibility. My dad, a pastor, says he sees the most trouble in parishioner relationships when in-laws can't figure out how to respect one another. My sister and her husband think it's important to share a taste in music. They say this to me as we sit in the open kitchen of the rented beach house where we're spending a week with our extended family; the soundtrack matters, of course, but so does the fact that we all genuinely enjoy one another.

My survey respondents, when asked about deal breakers, were less specific, and wiser, than I anticipated. Some said active addictions. Cruelty, racism, sexism, homophobia: these were other intolerable things. Nothing about the way they clip their toenails or the appropriate direction of the toilet paper roll. Most suggested that it was important to them that family and friends got along well with their partners. I asked two separate questions about the relative importance of shared interest in hobbies or activities and about the relative importance of shared political or religious beliefs. To those who hold deep religious or political convictions, it was important that those were largely shared; to those without strong religious or political convictions, it was more important that their partners share hobbies or interests. *How will you spend time together if you don't like the same things?* one asked.

Interestingly, most of the religious folks weren't particularly concerned that their partner share their religious tradition, only that they were similarly active or committed or even just open in their religious life. I know a number of clergy couples in which one spouse is Christian and the other partner is Jewish, Muslim, or Buddhist. I joke that I never successfully dated a Christian, despite my cradle-to-grave religious allegiances. Josh participates in Christian life and culture, but is sort of agnostic. Religiosity was a big part of our premarital counseling: I discovered that his support of my belief and willingness to raise the kids was more important to me than his professing a personal belief in the Risen Christ; he promised to always say nice things about Jesus, but wanted to retain the right to criticize the church for its periodically garbage way of being in the world.

Sometimes holidays are actually harder in relationships where both partners practice the same religion: when you date a Muslim, you never have to fight about whose family you're going to celebrate Christmas with. The rules, such as they are, for making a relationship work across religious difference are pretty much the same as making any relationship work: mutual respect of the partner's right to be different from you.

As we saw in chapter four, the worst part about being single, my survey respondents said, was the loneliness. One need not be single to experience loneliness, however. It's entirely possible to be lonely in a relationship, and that's probably a good sign that this pairing needs to either change or end.

PSYCHOLOGIST JOHN GOTTMAN has studied couples for years, bringing them into his "Love Lab" (which only *sounds* skeezy) to be interviewed. While they're interviewed, various physiological responses are monitored and measured. After years of research, Gottman suggested that there are two types of couples, those he calls the "masters" and the "disasters." The masters were happily together after years; the disasters had decided either to split or to live in misery. The physiology of each group differed drastically.

Emily Esfahani Smith, telling the story in *The Atlantic,* writes:

> The disasters looked calm during the interviews, but their physiology, measured by the electrodes, told a different story. Their heart rates were quick, their sweat glands were active, and their blood flow was fast. Following thousands of couples longitudinally, Gottman found that the more physiologically active the couples were in the lab, the quicker their relationships deteriorated over time.
>
> But what does physiology have to do with anything? The problem was that the disasters showed all the signs of arousal—of being in fight-or-flight mode—in their relationships. Having a conversation sitting next to their spouse was, to their bodies, like facing off with a saber-toothed tiger. Even when they were talking about pleasant or mundane facets of their relationships, they were prepared to attack and be attacked. This sent their heart rates soaring and made them more aggressive toward each other.[2]

The "masters," on the other hand, were physiologically at rest. Their bodies reflected that their relationships were havens of comfort, trust, and intimacy.

A haven is not a cave. Some introverted couples love just holing up together, while extroverted couples may need to be out in the world together. A haven of intimacy can travel. But how do you go about getting a haven?

Knowing what intimacy is and what intimate interactions look like constitutes a good start. Domeena Renshaw, now retired founding director of the Loyola Sex Therapy Clinic in Chicago, defines it in her supremely interesting volume *Seven Weeks to Better Sex* as "a closeness of your minds, your emotions, and your beliefs."[3]

Closeness, of course, doesn't look the same to everyone: I like to cuddle and pile and touch, basically constantly. I have not much in the way of personal space when it comes to loved ones. I am lucky that my beloved spouse is touchy-feely. My friend dated a guy who was content to come spend the night without anything sexual transpiring—he'd just spend the night in her bed—and she loved that. But she'd usually have her fill of the super-close cuddling after about three minutes and then have to come up with a kind and loving way to tell him to scoot over.

Intimate interaction isn't, then, just about a particular sort of closeness. Renshaw describes those interactions as "the seven Rs": respect, risk-taking, responsibility, rights, regard, reciprocity, and response.[4] Respect the other's needs and desires; take risks to try something new or say hard things, regardless of the consequences (how terrifying can it be to be the first to say "I love you"?); take responsibility for the

health of the relationship—both have to invest fully; honor
the other's right to things like privacy and honesty; assume
the worth of the partner and take an interest in his or her
well-being; be fair—he shouldn't get to go out drinking with
his friends and then gripe when she wants to go hang with
hers; and finally, respond to each other thoughtfully, and
when asked.[5]

The response one colored my friend's dilemma with the
wonderful cuddling guy. She didn't want to tell him to shove
off. She needed some more inches in the bed, but she loved
him and didn't want him to feel hurt.

Gottman's research on the masters and the disasters
reflects wisdom similar to that in Renshaw's work. In the
early nineties, Gottman created a retreat for 130 couples and
observed them on this "vacation" as they ate, hung out, and
relaxed. Over the course of the day, he charted how many
times one partner would make a "bid" for connection. The
bid could be about anything. *Hey, look at this cool bird! Listen
to this neat thing I'm reading.* The number of bids made was
telling—how much did the couple want to connect, even in
little ways, with each other? The partner's response was
another significant source of information. Did she respond
with interest, "turning toward" her partner and connecting with him? Did he basically ignore her, "turning away"?
Was she rude or hostile—*Can't you see I'm trying to read?*—
slamming the door on intimacy?

Couples that didn't make it had a lot fewer bids, and a
lot fewer connections. The happy couples bid more and responded more. They were connected, meeting each other's
emotional needs.

A relationship that's worth being in, the kind that doesn't leave you feeling more lonely than you were when you were single, but creates a sense of peace and even joy, is built on these interactions. Relationships thrive or perish based on how we connect with one another. The "masters of love" in Gottman's work are kind to each other. They do not express contempt, nor foster it. They are generous, not hostile or critical.

Though Josh isn't a Christian, when he and I started dating, I recognized in him a manifestation of the gospel—of trust and hope and forgiveness, of the abundance of love. He wasn't afraid of being nice to me—that I might read too much into it; he didn't see our relationship as a vying for power, or a competition.

There's a story in all four Gospels (that's rare, that a story appears in all four) in which Jesus has been teaching a crowd of people and it comes time to eat and they're all hungry and there's really nothing to eat. This is a crowd in the range of five thousand, too, not like twenty for a daylong conference. The disciples tell Jesus that the people are getting restless, and ask him what they should do. He instructs them to go around and ask everybody what they've got to share, and to see how much they get. So the disciples go around and ask everybody, and apparently no one assumed this teaching would go that long, because when they return to Jesus all they've collected is five loaves of bread and two fish. This is clearly not enough to feed everybody, even if the people are only getting Communion-size chunks and the disciples plan to serve the whole fish, bones and all.

Jesus prays over the food regardless and sends the

disciples out to distribute it. Miraculously, there is enough. More than enough. Somehow, there are leftovers.

I love this story. I love it because whether "God provides the increase," or whether the people felt inspired to cough up more than they'd initially offered to the kitty, this is a story about how trust and faith lead to abundance. We're all in this together, and when we come together, there's usually enough.

Masters of love know there's no danger of a love shortfall. Love begets love. Kindness leads to kindness. Trust demonstrated strengthens trust all around.

I WANTED TO be with Josh because (among 2,700 other reasons) he saw us right away as a team. Not a team against the world—not as Romeo and Juliet, who, romantic as they are, you'll recall, end up dead in the near term—just a team: in this together.

We've all known couples we knew weren't going to make it; some of us have even been a part of that kind of couple. He talks to her terribly; she berates his interests.

People are different. We're all different; we're all strangers to one another. But *how* we respond to difference, how we treat strangers and those dear to us, makes all the difference. Are we stingy with praise? Are we lousy at sharing? Josh loves—*loves*—fantasy football. He is commissioner of his league. He and our daughters speak longingly of the day, hopefully before the fulfillment of time, on which the league trophy will return to our home. Our daughters, in fact, referred to football as "Go, go, go!!!" in their early years, because their father routinely jumps out of his seat to wave his arms at "his" players and shout at them.

I do not quite understand this.

I am not athletic. I am not particularly competitive. I make, as you can imagine, a terrible sports fan. For my husband, Sundays from September through January or February are for football. He will come to church if I am preaching and he can record the games; he prefers to attend my dad's church during the season because it is closer to our home and they get done sooner.

For me, Sundays are for church and napping and family dinner.

I will not tell you that this difference has never been an issue for us. Soon after we started dating, Josh and his friends held their draft and after-party *on my birthday*. But we've figured out, over time, how to cross the chasm of our interests. Josh usually doesn't prioritize football over our family's needs: the girls have jerseys and watch with him. He, though an active viewer of televised games, is never rude or profane or overtly angry in their presence.

I don't get how he can spend hours each week watching football, how he can get so worked up about something that is supposed to be relaxing, that is, in the grand scheme of things, so inconsequential.

To be fair, he doesn't understand how I can get just as absorbed by a terrible book as a good one, or work on friendships and collegial relationships with people who annoy him.

Josh hasn't spent all day and night watching football and ignoring his family in forever. I haven't read a crappy novel instead of receiving one of his bids for connection in a while, either.

I once dated a guy who, while losing at a drinking game, punched a hole in a wall. I was shocked. He was a totally great guy, but that kind of anger—wherever it was coming from, and whatever it was really about—scared me. That was the beginning of the end of us, I think. I know that sometimes people are jerks about one thing, and that their poor behavior doesn't necessarily carry into other things. But I don't believe that with any conviction, not really. If someone is mean, it's only a matter of time before she's mean to you. If someone cheats to be with you, he'll probably cheat on you. Jesus says, "Whoever is faithful with little is also faithful with much, and the one who is dishonest with little is also dishonest with much" (Luke 16:10, CEB). Whoever gets that mad about a beer game will probably get mad over equally inconsequential things over time. I didn't think he'd ever hit me, but I wasn't overly inspired to stick around and find out.

That's not to say that people can't change. The "masters of love" in Gottman's work saw kindness as a muscle, one that strengthened with practice. We can learn to be more honest, more kind, more gracious. We can, in John Wesley's language, grow more perfect in love. With God's grace, we can do all things; nothing is impossible with God.

The promises we make to each other—either in weddings or well before—can be kept. There are tons of happy unions. Extended monogamy, contrary to what the armchair evolutionary biologists suggest, is totally possible and can be wildly fulfilling. But, as Renshaw suggests, both partners have to be all in.

My last serious relationship before Josh ended somewhat unilaterally; we were starting to look to the future together, and I realized—the way you know in the pit of your stomach—that I didn't want to be with him anymore. It wasn't anything about him. He was great. But I wasn't all in, and I didn't think I ever would be.

THERE'S GREAT DEBATE, wailing and gnashing of teeth, over the Disneyfication of our culture's ideas about love. You could draw it back to any number of sources, but I see it most clearly in the 1959 feature film *Sleeping Beauty*. After Maleficent casts her terrible spell and disappears with a cackle, Merryweather tries to soften the blow. *Not in death but just in sleep the fateful prophesy you'll keep . . . when true love's kiss the spell shall break.* Then the chorus sings: *For true love conquers all.*

Love is all you need, the Beatles sang not long after that.

We, the wizened, may not always believe that. We've been hurt. Those sentiments are for pop songs and children. But for Christians, our critique ignores the roots of these convictions in our own funny culture, in our own scriptures. It's rendered this way in 1 John: "There is no fear in love, but perfect love casts out fear" (4:18). The Song of Songs proclaims, "for love is strong as death, passion fierce as the grave" (8:6). It's in Romans like this:

> No, in all these things we are more than conquerors through him who loved us. For I am convinced that neither death, nor life, nor angels, nor rulers, nor things present, nor things to come, nor powers, nor height, nor depth, nor anything else in all

creation, will be able to separate us from the love
of God in Christ Jesus our Lord.

(8:37–39)

Come what may . . . true love conquers all . . .
Love is of God. I believe that. Love is one of the primary
ways that we know God, that we recognize God. And love
can empower us to do more than we ever thought possible:
to work for healing, for better ways of living and being in
relationship.

People, though, not being God, need not only love but also
the practices—or the skills—of loving well. To move the moti-
vation to reconcile or change into action. Writer Ann Patchett,
in the titular essay of her recent collection *This Is the Story of
a Happy Marriage,* describes the "unmitigated disaster"[6] of her
first marriage. "Oddly, what I fell back on during that time
were the lessons of my high school home economics classes.
I decided I would maintain stability through food prepara-
tion. . . . We drank huge quantities of milk."[7]

She was going to fix him, make him just how she wanted
him. But he resented her, did not treasure her efforts or
who she was. She could find no exits, could not see that "the
world wouldn't end were I to pack up and leave."[8]

Finally, she found a way out. She had an affair. She seeks
no absolution; things got worse, much worse, before they got
better. In the middle of that, she meets a woman who has
recently divorced. This woman asks her:

"Does your husband make you a better person? . . .
Are you smarter, kinder, more generous, more

compassionate, a better writer? . . . Does he make you better?"

"That's not the question," I said. "It's so much more complicated than that."

"It's not more complicated than that," she said.

"That's all there is: Does he make you better and do you make him better?"[9]

When Ann eventually leaves her husband, she calls her mother, who says, "What took you so long?" Everyone could see it but Ann and her husband.

Not everyone leaves. Some people stay and make each other miserable for years. All things being equal, I think God would prefer that those couples find healing as individuals that would allow them to reconcile as pairs. God wants us to honor our commitments. God wants us to hope for change. But sometimes we are unable to work with God in the context of a given relationship. Sometimes one of us is, but our partner isn't. Sometimes a partner won't take responsibility for his or her role in a relationship.

A few years ago, there was another article in *The Atlantic* that made a bit of a splash. "Marry Him!" Lori Gottlieb instructed women. The question stands before every woman over thirty-five: "Is it better to be alone, or to settle?"

> My advice is this: Settle! That's right. Don't worry about passion or intense connection. Don't nix a guy based on his annoying habit of yelling "Bravo!" in movie theaters. Overlook his halitosis or abysmal sense of aesthetics. Because if you want to

have the infrastructure in place to have a family, settling is the way to go. Based on my observations, in fact, settling will probably make you happier in the long run, since many of those who marry with great expectations become more disillusioned with each passing year. (It's hard to maintain that level of *zing* when the conversation morphs into discussions about who's changing the diapers or balancing the checkbook.)[10]

Gottlieb writes as a single mother—a woman who wanted to be mother and went ahead and had a baby despite never having found Mr. Right. There are things she's right about: if you want a family, and you want a marriage, you will be well served by reminding yourself that nobody's perfect. My husband likes beef jerky. I have seen him eat something called a "pickled sausage" that he purchased at a gas station. He, the poor man, has to live with someone who is right about everything, all the time, at least in her own humble opinion. I also have both failed to lose all the baby weight after our third child and steadfastly refuse to reduce my sugar or alcohol intake, much less take up running. (I hate running.)

Nobody's perfect. But we try to be kind to each other. I try to be nice when his gas station purchase wreaks digestive havoc. He signs me up with Fitbit and MyFitnessPal and cooks healthy recipes for dinner, because he loves me and does not want me to develop diabetes. He also does not gloat about his much higher metabolism.

Gottlieb's wrong about settling, though. Imperfect people can have successful, intimate relationships, but no matter how perfect two people seem to be for each other, if they're not both all in, it'll never work. The state of being fully committed to a relationship is synonymous with actually doing the work of being in a relationship. A couple I know does not want to split, but he gets mad whenever asked to care for their children, speaks harshly to her, and flirts with others. He's still there, but he's not living into the commitment they made to each other.

When a relationship ends, especially one that's lasted awhile and been intimate, one that's had good times as well as bad, there's bound to be grief. But grief doesn't always mean the decision was a bad one. Leaving someone who doesn't love you or who hurts you or even someone you can't commit to for one reason or another is fraught, but sometimes it's necessary.

At the same time, I am amazed—profoundly grateful and amazed—by stories of couples who have made their relationships last through thick and thin, through sickness and health, through richer and poorer. Lost jobs, grad school stress, cross-country moves, illness, poverty, mental illness, recovery, terrible bosses, infidelity both physical and emotional, feuding families. People make it work all the time.

It's kind of a miracle, and I'm not always sure how it works. But, like the loaves and the fishes, I'm pretty sure it has something to do with the fact that the important things in life are ours in abundance, and can never run short: kindness, trust, love, and generosity are the gifts that keep on giving. Christians can and should claim this truth. We love, because God first loved us.

If you share your love with someone who cannot or does not reciprocate, it's over.

But if you share your love in risk and trust, and that person loves you back with hope and kindness, you're well on your way. After all, the poet writes, "Many waters cannot quench love / neither can floods drown it" (Song of Songs 8:7).

Afterword

The Nature of Love

I f I first learned about sex from books, I first learned about love from music. My dad listened to the Beatles and all the hits of the sixties; my mother to Broadway musicals, old and new. I am forever amazed by the endless wealth of songs that speak to this marvelous, risk-filled, life-giving, mope-inspiring human endeavor.

I listened to the Paul Simon station on Pandora as I got started on this book, but eventually I switched over to the station based on the song "La Vie en rose," a staple of the Great American Songbook (despite being French). The singer speaks of how the world is transformed through love, through the presence of the beloved: the world is magic, colored by roses. *Everyday words seem to turn into love songs.*[1]

Torch songs help with the composition of pages about love. This is my primary discovery in writing this book.

There are those who would rather Christians stop writing, and speaking, and preaching about sex. Some think addressing the topic plays into the obsessions of our sex-saturated culture; some think we can't keep ourselves from moralizing and are making a terrible name for ourselves. Some think such discussion simply pushes the limits of propriety. Some think sex has no real bearing on the substantive theological and ethical concerns of the tradition.

I don't count myself among any of those people, obviously, though I do wish—along with the bulk of my survey respondents—that religious people, if they must speak of sex, would cease and desist in the propagation of terrible theology and bigotry. Since that seems unlikely, however, the burden falls to other Christians to offer a more fulsome account of how Christianity might understand human sexuality.

My hope for this book is not simply a defensive one, though. As a Christian, I want to be both as wise as a serpent and as innocent as a dove; I want to see the world through the eyes of truth and love; I want to live *la vie en rose*.

The words of scripture illuminating the steadfast presence of a loving God, the life, death, and resurrection of Jesus Christ, the work of the Holy Spirit: all these point to a world shaped, moved, and transformed by love.

Love is not synonymous with sex, but they are closely intertwined. The grace of being seen and known, of being vulnerable and welcomed into the life and body of another, is often present in both. The passion that inspires us to participate in the world and in relationship with others is present in eros, the erotic love that drives us to seek out and share our selves with a partner.

It's not just Louis Armstrong and Ella Fitzgerald and Frank Sinatra and Billie Holiday who have shaped my understanding of love, of course. I'm a Methodist preacher's kid, which means I grew up with a steady diet of Charles Wesley hymns. I once got a hymnal *for my birthday*.

The first hymn—the first hymn in every edition of the Methodist hymnal ever—is "O, for a Thousand Tongues to Sing." There are roughly a million verses, but the one that's helped me to make sense of the gospel for years and years is this one:

In Christ your Head, you then shall know,
Shall feel your sins forgiven;
Anticipate your heaven below,
And own that love is heaven.[2]

Anticipate heaven: know, own, that love is heaven. The fulfillment of life with God in the fullness of time is love.

Charles Wesley was possibly incapable of writing short hymns. Another epically long one, "Come, O Thou Traveler Unknown," tells the story of Jacob (who became Israel) wrestling with the messenger of God. *Tell me your name*, Jacob asks, *and I will let you go*. Wesley takes the story and places it in the larger context of God's story.

Tis Love! 'tis Love! Thou diedst for me!
I hear Thy whisper in my heart;

The morning breaks, the shadows flee,
Pure, universal love Thou art;
To me, to all, Thy bowels move;
Thy nature and Thy Name is Love.[3]

The nature of God—the name of God—is love: and we wrestle with it forever. The way we come to understand and see ourselves, God, and our neighbors is through wrestling with love.

Wrestling, dancing, weaving in and out, grappling and grabbing, moving and repositioning: these are verbs of metaphor with an abstract and mysterious God. But they are also descriptive of seduction, erotic discovery, and sexual relationships.

Sex marks us; love changes us. So does God. Jacob ends up with a name change and a wrenched hip. The risk of those marks, of that change, can be frightening or exhilarating, but neither justifies avoidance. Sex is like nitroglycerin, after all: capable of healing hearts and blowing up bridges. It's powerful, and holy.

Powerful things, holy things, scare us to death, individually and culturally. We draw a lot of lines in the sand, and we wag a lot of fingers, trying to protect ourselves, trying to render sex and love less potent, less dangerous, through tsk-tsking and legislation. We condemn a lot of people, ignoring logs in our own eyes.

Sex and love, though, can be key experiences of the truth of Jesus's words: that those who would save their lives will lose them and those who would lose their lives will save them. (Paul Simon captures the sentiment in other words in his melancholic song, "I Am a Rock."[4]) Jesus dies, we might try to recall when we are most afraid, and rises again. Death and sin have no victory for us.

Sex, Love, Life: these cannot be separated from one another. The greatest commandment is to love self, God, and neighbor with all that we are; the vocation we all share is to learn how to be in relationship with God, with ourselves, with one another. It's terribly simple; it's harder than it sounds.

The poets and crooners nail it, as always:

You've got to give a little, take a little,
And let your poor heart break a little.
That's the story of, that's the glory of love.[5]

Acknowledgments

A cknowledging the people who contributed to the researching and writing of a book is always difficult; acknowledging the people who made possible a book you've been, in one way or another, writing for years and years seems particularly important and daunting.

Many, many thanks . . .

First, to my parents, Brett and Lauri. I can't even believe how lucky I am to have you, as models and guides and sources of endless, undeserved, loving support. I try to be like you, you know. Thank you for being proud of me, even though I wrote a book about sex.

To my sisters, Whitney and Taylor. Growing up in a house full of girls was a great and wondrous gift, and I am who I am because of you. I love you, and your dear husbands, and your children.

To my grandparents Jean and Al. For sharing your stories and believing in me always as a writer, thinker, and religious leader. Thank you for your love of books and all those newspaper clippings, and for your love, affection, delight, and periodic bemusement with each other. It can be hard to be married to a perfect person, but you both do it so well.

To my grandparents Dorothy and Bert, who rest with God. For bearing witness to the romantic charge that can bind two people together over the decades. We miss you.

To my beloved, of course, for creating the space and time for me to write this book. For believing that this is important work for the church, for believing our daughters deserve to live and love in a culture that does better than the one we've currently got.

To John, my father-in-law, without whose support, washing of dishes, and caring for children, this book would absolutely not have gotten written. I know you think those constant hours of playing with our children so Josh and I could escape to the library amount to very little. But you are wrong.

To Fiona, Calliope, and Henrietta: my prayer is not that you avoid deep embarrassment over your mother's writing about these things, because who am I kidding, but rather that this book will demonstrate to you that I am here to talk about whatever you need to talk about, always.

To the boys I loved and longed for, once upon a time. It is silly to lump you together, except in this: you have been uniformly gracious about this project, and for that I offer many thanks. It's a privilege to have known you, and a delight to hear how your lives have unfolded since last we met.

To Cynthia Lindner, mentor and friend, who, when I

lamented the release of a pastoral book about sexuality years before I was ready to write one, said, "Don't worry. You'll write yours eventually, and it will be better." For all the books (I still have your Foucault) and the conversations, I am eternally grateful.

To Anne Hampson, L.C.P.C., whose wisdom contributed to what I hope is a wise book.

To staff and students at Rockefeller Memorial Chapel, Spiritual Life, and the Divinity School at the University of Chicago, especially Tahir Abdullah, Elizabeth Davenport, Rachel Heath, and Jigna Shah in the office, and students Emily Anagnostos, George Arcenaux, Leah Challberg, McKinna Daugherty, Joe Hopkins, Katie Kuntz-Wineland, Tonks Lynch, and Kiva Nice-Webb. For listening to me process, for reading drafts, for enduring more sermons than strictly necessary on sexuality, for distributing and taking my survey, for graciously offering time off to finish. For sharing your own stories and believing this book is important for both young adults and public religion.

To the Sunday morning worshipping congregation at Rockefeller, thank you for your enthusiasm for our ministry together.

To the people of Union Church of Hinsdale, and Senior Pastor Mike Solberg. We are just beginning our ministry together, but I am so grateful you are supportive of writing as a part of my vocational life. I could make do with a little less teasing about the content of this book.

To Kris Culp and Yvonne Gilmore of Disciples Divinity House and Stacy Alan of Brent House, both at U of C, for having me to speak with your communities about this work, and for countless conversations about these topics. Also for your friendship.

To William Schweiker, who was among the first to read my attempts to link Wesley, Tillich, and human sexuality nearly a decade ago, and reminded me that I shouldn't leave out considerations of concupiscence.

To my writer/pastor friends: Rebecca Anderson, Magrey de Vega, Ben Dueholm, Heidi Haverkamp, Lee Hull Moses, Sandhya Jha, Jenn Moland-Kovash, Kyle Rader, Danya Ruttenberg, Erica Schemper, Wesley Sun, Laura Jean Torgerson, and Katherine Willis Pershey. Writing would be lonely and this book would have suffered dreadfully without your eyes on chapters, ears for ideas, and heart for this project. Thank you all.

To the members of the Young Clergy Women Project, for your support, enthusiasm, and ministry.

To other writer/religious types, namely Amy Frykholm, Jessica Miller Kelley, and Steve Thorngate, for opportunities to write and think through issues of love, sex, and faith—and how you write about them—with you.

To Lil Copan, who's gone to bat for this project from the beginning.

To Lauren Winner, editor extraordinaire, who, among her many other gifts, helped this book to be all it could be.

To Carol Mann for taking me on and finding this book such a wonderful home.

To Kathryn Hamilton and all the marvelous people at HarperOne.

To all who took the survey, you are so brave, and I hope this text does your stories justice.

Notes

INTRODUCTION: ON SEX AND CHRISTIANS
1. Frederick Buechner, *Wishful Thinking,* rev. ed. (San Francisco: HarperOne, 1993), 107.

CHAPTER ONE: "MY FAVORITE FEEL"
1. Ha.
2. Joanna Cole, *Asking About Sex and Growing Up: A Question-and-Answer Book for Boys and Girls* (New York: Morrow Junior Books, 1988), 40.
3. Cole, *Asking About Sex and Growing Up,* 41.
4. Feminism in the United States has been, for generations, limited by its lack of attention to the needs, wisdom, and stories of women of color. Intersectionality is critically important for those of us doing this work going forward.

5. Sara Moslener talks about this in great detail in her important study *Virgin Nation: Sexual Purity and American Adolescence* (Oxford: Oxford University Press, 2015).
6. Saint Augustine, *Confessions*, trans. Garry Wills (New York: Penguin, 2002), 173.
7. Kyle Rader, recent Ph.D. in Theology, The University of Chicago, totally brilliant. Somebody give him a tenure-track position.
8. Christine Gudorf, *Body, Sex, and Pleasure: Reconstructing Christian Sexual Ethics* (Cleveland: Pilgrim Press, 1994), 92.
9. Gudorf, *Body, Sex, and Pleasure*, 89.
10. Gudorf, *Body, Sex, and Pleasure*, 90.
11. Gudorf, *Body, Sex, and Pleasure*, 91.
12. Caitlin Moran, *How to Be a Woman* (New York: Harper Perennial, 2011), 15.
13. Moran, *How to Be a Woman*, 25.
14. Moran, *How to Be a Woman*, 27.
15. Moran, *How to Be a Woman*, 26.
16. Cole, *Asking About Sex and Growing Up*, 42.
17. Moran, *How to Be a Woman*, 30.
18. Gudorf, *Body, Sex, and Pleasure*, 94.
19. Gudorf, *Body, Sex, and Pleasure*, 94.

CHAPTER TWO: FIRSTS

1. ConAgra Foods, which makes and sells Swiss Miss, is fairly categorized as "Big Food" and is complicit in a lot of the sins of that industry—environmental, and labor. We should all really only be consuming fair-trade chocolate.
2. Sebastian Moore, "The Crisis of an Ethic Without Desire," in *Theology and Sexuality: Classic and Contemporary*

Readings, ed. Eugene F. Rogers, Jr. (Oxford: Blackwell Publishers, 2002), 160.

3. Moore, "Crisis of an Ethic," 160.
4. Moore, "Crisis of an Ethic," 160.
5. "The Nearness of You," written in 1938 by Hoagy Carmichael with lyrics by Ned Washington, and covered by absolutely everyone since then. My favorite version is by Norah Jones.
6. Rainbow Rowell, *Eleanor & Park* (New York: St. Martin's Griffin, 2013).
7. "I Only Have Eyes For You" is a great song: www.youtube.com/watch?v=63nlhoda2MY.
8. Paul Tillich, "You Are Accepted!" in *The Shaking of the Foundations* (New York: Charles Scribner's Sons, 1948), 153–63.
9. Rowan D. Williams, "The Body's Grace," in *Theology and Sexuality,* ed. Rogers, 311–12.
10. This is what always irked me about some friends who did psychotropic drugs in college and suggested it made them better writers or poets, that it helped them understand the world in ways non-acid-dropping me never could.
11. John Wesley, "The Means of Grace" in *John Wesley's Sermons,* eds. Albert C. Outler and Richard P. Heitzenrater (Nashville: Abingdon Press, 1991), 157.
12. Jim Hancock and Kara Eckmann Powell, *Good Sex: A Whole-Person Approach to Teenage Sexuality and God* (Grand Rapids, MI: Zondervan, 2001), 9.
13. Moore, "Crisis of an Ethic," 158.
14. Moore, "Crisis of an Ethic," 158.

CHAPTER THREE: PLAYING FAIR

1. First sign of a call to ministry? An inability to make small talk. Within ten seconds of meeting someone, I'll be asking about his work, studies, passions, family, commitments . . .

2. That's a synonym for "horny," a word I totally hate.

3. Paula Fredriksen, Sin: The Early History of an Idea (Princeton: Princeton Univ. Press: 2012), 1–2.

4. James B. Nelson, "Where Are We? Seven Sinful Problems and Seven Virtuous Possibilities" in Perspectives on Marriage: A Reader, eds. Kieran Scott and Michael Warren (New York: Oxford Univ. Press, 2001), 177.

5. Frederick Buechner, patron saint of literary-minded mainliners, has a fabulous micro-essay on the Bible in Wishful Thinking that concludes with this metaphor: "If you look at a window, you see flyspecks, dust, the crack where Junior's Frisbee hit it. If you look through a window, you see the world beyond. Something like this is the difference between those who see the Bible as a Holy Bore and those who see it as the Word of God, which speaks out of the depths of an almost unimaginable past into the depths of ourselves." Wishful Thinking, 12.

6. For example: The two books each of Kings and Chronicles record different perspectives on the same period of time in Israel's and Judah's histories, and they don't always agree. Also, there are four canonical Gospels, and Jesus only lived once.

7. Proof-texting is basically picking biblical verses out of their context and stringing them together to support an argument, without regard for whether or not the

intended meaning of the verses or passages is particularly honored.

8. Martin Buber, *I and Thou,* 2nd ed. (New York: Charles
   Scribner's Sons, 1958).

9. The marvelous collection of essays entitled *The
   Passionate Torah: Sex and Judaism,* edited by Danya
   Ruttenberg (New York: New York Univ. Press, 2009), is
   structured around Buber's *I and Thou.* I owe a great deal
   to Rabbi Ruttenberg's thought and work.

10. Which is not to say that we ought to be careless with
    the things we use. We shouldn't leave the spoon to grow
    mold on our desks or chuck it into the garbage disposal.
    But a thing is categorically different from a person.

11. Biblical scholars mostly agree that the writers of
    Matthew and Luke shared quite a bit of source material,
    though they order things differently.

12. Margaret Farley, *Just Love: A Framework for Christian
    Sexual Ethics* (New York: Continuum, 2008), 184.

13. "Vatican Critiques Book by Mercy Sister Margaret Farley,"
    news release, United States Conference of Catholic
    Bishops, June 4, 2012, www.usccb.org/news/2012/12–097
    .cfm.

14. Farley, *Just Love,* 231.

15. Melanie Springer Mock, "True Love Consents: Why
    Teach Christian Youth About Boundaries," *her.meneu-
    tics* (blog), *Christianity Today,* November 23, 2015, www
    .christianitytoday.com/women/2015/november/true
    -love-consents.html?paging=off.

16. Springer Mock, "True Love Consents."

17. Kory Plockmeyer, "The Place of Consent in a Christian

Sexual Ethic," *Think Christian,* June 12, 2013, http:// thinkchristian.reframemedia.com/the-place-of-consent -in-a-christian-sexual-ethic.

18. Conor Friedersdorf, "When 'Do Unto Others' Meets Hookup Culture: How Christians Could Talk to America About Sex," *The Atlantic,* September 10, 2014, www.theatlantic.com/politics/archive/2014/09/how -christians-could-talk-to-america-about-sex/375628/.

19. Friedersdorf, "When 'Do Unto Others.'"

20. Farley, *Just Love,* 207.

CHAPTER FOUR: SINGLENESS, SEX, AND WAITING

1. Wendy Wang and Kim Parker, "Record Share of Americans Have Never Married as Values, Economics and Gender Patterns Change," Pew Research Center, September 24, 2014, www.pewsocialtrends.org/2014 /09/24/record-share-of-americans-have-never-married/.

2. There are any number of books which evidence some of these ideas. See *When God Writes Your Love Story,* by Eric and Leslie Ludy; *I Kissed Dating Goodbye,* by Josh Harris; or *Before You Meet Prince Charming,* by Sarah Mally, for example.

3. Process theology challenges some of the classical formulations of God as immutable, immortal, and impassable and instead suggests that God can be affected by the happenings of the world and, indeed, changes, influencing the world, moving us toward love.

4. Alfred North Whitehead, *Process and Reality* (New York: The Free Press, 1978), 29.

5. Tanzila Ahmed, "Can I Get a Witness?" *Love InshAllah,*

November 4, 2015, http://loveinshallah.com/2015/11/04
/can-i-get-a-witness/.

6. Dale Martin, *Sex and the Single Savior: Gender and
Sexuality in Biblical Interpretation* (Louisville, KY:
Westminster John Knox, 2006), 91.

CHAPTER FIVE: NAKED

1. Naomi Seidman, "The Erotics of Sexual Segregation" in
The Passionate Torah, ed. Danya Ruttenberg, 112.

2. Mindy Spradlin, "5 Lies I Learned About Sex Growing
Up in Church Culture," December 27, 2015, www.mindy
spradlin.com/blog-1/2015/12/27/5-lies-i-learned-about
-sex-from-the-church.

3. Mark and Grace Driscoll, *Real Marriage: The Truth About
Sex, Friendship, and Life Together* (Nashville: Thomas
Nelson, 2012), 9.

4. "In forgiving and walking with Grace . . ." I seriously
hope he's forgiving her for concealing her infidelity and
not anything related to her assault, but this passage sort
of suggests the latter. Which is one of a hundred thousand ways this book is crazy. Driscoll and Driscoll, *Real
Marriage*, 16.

5. Driscoll and Driscoll, *Real Marriage*, 12–17.

6. Karen Lebacqz, "Appropriate Vulnerability: A Sexual
Ethic for Singles" in *Sexuality and the Sacred: Sources for
Theological Reflection*, 2nd ed., ed. Marvin M. Ellison and
Kelly Brown Douglas (Louisville, KY: Westminster John
Knox, 2010), 274.

7. Lebacqz, *Sexuality and the Sacred*, 274.

8. Lebacqz, *Sexuality and the Sacred*, 275.

9. Lebacqz, *Sexuality and the Sacred*, 275.
10. Lebacqz, *Sexuality and the Sacred*, 275.
11. Seidman, "The Erotics of Sexual Segregation," 108.
12. Seidman, "The Erotics of Sexual Segregation," 109.
13. Billy Collins, "Man in Space," in *The Art of Drowning* (Pittsburgh: University of Pittsburgh Press, 1995), 68.
14. Rebecca Solnit, *Men Explain Things to Me* (Chicago: Haymarket Books, 2014), 1–16.
15. Billy Collins, "Victoria's Secret," in *Picnic, Lightning* (Pittsburgh: University of Pittsburgh Press, 1998), 55–58.
16. John Green, *The Fault in Our Stars* (New York: Dutton Books, 2012), 206.
17. Mary Oliver, "I Did Think, Let's Go About This Slowly," in *Felicity* (New York: Penguin, 2015), 51.

CHAPTER SIX: WE MIGHT BE STRANGERS

1. Ani DiFranco, "Independence Day," from *Little Plastic Castle*, Righteous Babe Records, 1998.
2. Cited in Bernard McGinn, "The Language of Love in Christian and Jewish Mysticism," in *Mysticism and Language*, ed. Steven Katz (Oxford: Oxford University Press, 1992), 204.
3. McGinn, "The Language of Love," 210.
4. McGinn, "The Language of Love," 210.
5. Paul Tillich, *Systematic Theology*, vol. 1 (Chicago: University of Chicago Press, 1951), 172.
6. Quoted in Diane Ackerman, *A Natural History of Love* (New York: Random House, 1994), 244.
7. Harriet Lerner, *The Dance of Intimacy: A Woman's Guide to Courageous Acts of Change in Key Relationships* (New York: Harper Perennial, 1989), 3.

8. Lerner, *The Dance of Intimacy*, 71.

9. Lerner, *The Dance of Intimacy*, 85.

10. A number of my survey respondents noted that they don't use pornography because they object to how it is made; that is, there are systemic injustices in the work of making porn that they can't get on board with. I was pleased to see that. That's a different objection, though, than abstaining to it because of the threat of addiction or other unhealthy distancing from healthy intimate relationships.

11. Here's just one of surely a million: www.chicagoreader.com /chicago/dan-savage-love-testicles-masturbation-erections -college/Content?oid = 6862503.

12. Gudorf, *Body, Sex, and Pleasure*, 106.

13. Gudorf, *Body, Sex, and Pleasure*, 105.

14. Gudorf, *Body, Sex, and Pleasure*, 109.

15. Donna Freitas, *Sex and the Soul: Juggling Sexuality, Spirituality, Romance, and Religion on America's College Campuses* (New York: Oxford University Press, 2008).

16. Donna Freitas, *The End of Sex: How Hookup Culture Is Leaving a Generation Unhappy, Sexually Unfulfilled, and Confused About Intimacy* (New York: Basic Books, 2013).

17. And only rarely should we. Get yourself tested, and use protection. Sex should not be death-dealing or a vector of infectious suffering.

18. Gudorf, *Body, Sex, and Pleasure*, 109.

CHAPTER SEVEN: HISTORY

1. Bob Dylan, "Most of the Time." Lyrics on his website: http://bobdylan.com/songs/most-time/.

2. Walt Bogdanich, "Reporting Rape and Wishing She Hadn't: How One College Handled a Sexual Assault Complaint," *New York Times*, July 12, 2014, www.nytimes .com/2014/07/13/us/how-one-college-handled-a-sexual -assault-complaint.html?_r = 0.

3. Simon van Zuylen-Wood, "Rape Happens Here," *Philadelphia* magazine, April 24, 2014, www.phillymag.com/articles /rape-happens-here-swarthmore-college-sexual-assaults/.

4. Renita J. Weems, *Battered Love: Marriage, Sex, and Violence in the Hebrew Prophets,* (Minneapolis: Fortress Press, 1995).

5. Van Zuylen-Wood, "Rape Happens Here."

6. John Wesley, "The Scripture Way of Salvation," in *John Wesley's Sermons,* eds. Outler and Heitzenrater.

7. Amy Frykholm, *See Me Naked: Stories of Sexual Exile in American Christianity* (Boston: Beacon Press, 2011), 22.

8. Frykholm, *See Me Naked,* 23.

9. Frykholm, *See Me Naked,* 24–26.

10. Frykholm, *See Me Naked,* 29.

11. Wesley, "The Scripture Way of Salvation," 372.

12. Wesley talked about "prevenient grace," as the grace that comes before—before we are even aware of it working in our lives or world.

13. Frykholm, *See Me Naked,* 24.

14. Wesley, "The Scripture Way of Salvation," 373.

15. Wesley, "The Scripture Way of Salvation," 375.

CHAPTER EIGHT: BE FAITHFUL

1. See, e.g., Courtney Reissig, "Good Sex Comes to Those Who Wait?" *Christianity Today,* July 10, 2014, www.christianitytoday.com/women/2014/july

/good-sex-comes-to-those-who-wait.html and Seth Adam
Smith, "Marriage Isn't for You," *Huffpost Weddings* (blog),
www.huffingtonpost.com/seth-adam-smith/marriage
-isnt-for-you_b_4209837.html.

2. Madeleine L'Engle, *The Irrational Season* (San Francisco:
HarperSanFrancisco, 1977), 49–50.

3. Esther Perel, *Mating in Captivity: Unlocking Erotic
Intelligence* (New York: Harper, 2006), xiv.

4. L'Engle, *The Irrational Season,* 49.

5. Kara Powell and Jim Hancock, *Good Sex: A Whole-Person
Approach to Teenage Sexuality and God* (Grand Rapids,
MI: Zondervan / Youth Specialties, 2001).

6. Simon Blackburn, *Lust: The Seven Deadly Sins* (New York:
Oxford Univ. Press, 2003), 2.

7. Farley, *Just Love,* 171.

8. Blackburn, *Lust,* 13.

9. Marc O'Brien, "On Seeing a Sex Surrogate," in *Stubborn
Light: The Best of the Sun,* vol. 3, ed. Sy Safransky (Chapel
Hill, NC: The Sun Publishing Co., 2000), 25.

10. O'Brien, "On Seeing a Sex Surrogate," 26.

11. O'Brien, "On Seeing a Sex Surrogate," 30.

12. D. H. Lawrence, "Wild Things in Captivity," reprinted as
the epigraph in Perel, *Mating in Captivity.*

13. Lawrence, "Wild Things in Captivity."

14. Perel, *Mating in Captivity,* 11.

15. Perel, *Mating in Captivity,* xviii.

CHAPTER NINE: THE AVOIDABLE AND THE INEVITABLE

1. Dietrich Bonhoeffer, *Letters & Papers from Prison* (New
York: Simon & Schuster, 1997), 43.

2. Emily Esfahani Smith, "Masters of Love," *The Atlantic*, June 12, 2014, www.theatlantic.com/health/archive /2014/06/happily-ever-after/372573/.

3. Domeena Renshaw, with Pam Brick, *Seven Weeks to Better Sex* (New York: Random House, 1995), 89.

4. Renshaw, *Seven Weeks to Better Sex*, 89.

5. Renshaw, *Seven Weeks to Better Sex*, 89–90.

6. Ann Patchett, *This Is the Story of a Happy Marriage* (New York: Harper, 2013), 246.

7. Patchett, *This Is the Story*, 247.

8. Patchett, *This Is the Story*, 245.

9. Patchett, *This Is the Story*, 249.

10. Lori Gottlieb, "Marry Him! The Case for Settling for Mr. Good Enough," *The Atlantic*, March 2008, www.theatlantic .com/magazine/archive/2008/03/marry-him/306651/.

AFTERWORD: THE NATURE OF LOVE

1. Édith Piaf, "La Vie en rose," written in 1945.

2. Charles Wesley, "O, for a Thousand Tongues to Sing" in *The United Methodist Hymnal* (Nashville: Abingdon, 1989), 57.

3. Charles Wesley, "Come, O Thou Traveler Unknown," in *The United Methodist Hymnal*, 386–7.

4. The lyrics are here: http://www.paulsimon.com/en-ca /track/i-am-a-rock-3.

5. Billy Hill, "The Glory of Love," first recorded by Benny Goodman in 1936.